Understanding Hearing Loss

Understanding Hearing Loss

Kenneth Lysons

Jessica Kingsley Publishers
London and Bristol, Pennsylvania

First published in the United Kingdom in 1996 by
Jessica Kingsley Publishers Ltd
116 Pentonville Road
London N1 9JB, England
and
1900 Frost Road, Suite 101
Bristol, PA 19007, U S A

Library of Congress Cataloging in Publication Data
Lysons, Kenneth.
Understanding hearing loss/Kenneth Lysons
p.cm.
Includes index
ISBN 185302–214–4 (pbk.)
1. Deafness--Popular works. 2. Patient education. I. Title
RF59.L96 1995
617.8--dc20

British Library Cataloguing in Publication Data
Lysons, Kenneth
Understanding Hearing Loss
I. Title
362.42

ISBN 185302 214 4

Printed and Bound in Great Britain by
Cromwell Press, Melksham, Wiltshire

Contents

Dedication   vii

Acknowledgements   viii

Introduction   ix

1. The Mechanism of Hearing   1

2. Some Causes of Hearing Loss   7

3. Measuring Hearing and Hearing Loss   21

4. You and Your Otologist   49

5. Hearing Impairment is More than Dull Ears   67

6. Hearing Aids and Other Devices   77

7. Cochlear Implants   108

8. Lipreading, Hearing Tactics and Auditory Training   120

9. Employment, Hospitalization and Family Relationships 137

10. Statutory and Voluntary Services for People with Impaired Hearing   149

Appendix 1. Hearing aid Council Code of Practice   158

Appendix 2. Form of Agreement for Supply of Hearing Aid(s)   166

Appendix 3. Some Useful Organizations 167

Index   171

Dedication

To Audrey, Michael, Jeffery and Edith. To my friends Gordon and Jeanne Ashton and Peter Werth – a small appreciation of his kindness.

Acknowledgements

In writing this book I have, to adapt a phrase of Charles Reade's, 'filled my bucket from many taps'. It would be impracticable to mention by name all those who have provided information or given advice. There are, however, a number of people to whom I am especially indebted.

Alison Heath of the National Association of Deafened People kindly contributed the autobiographical account of her experience with cochlea implants in Chapter 7.

Judith Hunt, then Secretary to the British Society of Hearing Therapists, went to much trouble in sending me information, some of which may provide a basis for further research.

Dr Ron McCaig of the Health and Safety Executive gave much help in connection with an intended Chapter on Noise and on industrial deafness which, for reasons of space has been omitted.

Mary Plackett, the Librarian to the RNID, has over the years, dealt patiently, courteously and competently with the writer's requests for information in connection with previous books. Her help has again been invaluable.

Brian Simpson of the Birmingham Resource Centre for Deafened People was a great source of encouragement and never failed to respond positively to requests for help. Dr Katarina Sherbourne, Course Co-ordinator of the Link Centre for Deafened People also provided useful information. Peter Werth, Chairman of PC Werth Ltd took an interest in the book from the outset and, after reading Chapter 6 in draft, made many constructive comments. The writer was fortunate in having such expert help in endeavouring to provide up to date information regarding an aspect of hearing rehabilitation in which improvements are continually being made.

Finally, Jeanne Ashton has once again helped with some of the research. The manuscript has been expertly text processed by Margaret Dudley, Edith Jones, Margaret Reid and Madeline Thompson.

Introduction

This book is intended for anyone who is hard of hearing or deafened or thinks he or she will become so; for anyone who lives or works with people who have a significant hearing loss; and for all who wish to know something about hearing disability and how it may be helped.

Three categories of hearing loss are covered by the terms 'deaf' and 'hard of hearing'. Since, in ordinary speech, we use the word 'deaf' indiscriminately to cover all types of hearing loss irrespective of its cause, age of onset or severity, it is important at the outset to distinguish between persons who are deaf, deafened, or hard of hearing.

People who are *deaf* are those whose sense of hearing is non-functional for the ordinary purposes of life. People in this category have little or no *usable* hearing. From the standpoints of education and social services, the distinction between *pre-lingual* and *post-lingual* deafness is particularly important. The former relates to the condition of persons whose deafness 'was present at birth or occurred at an age prior to the development of speech and language'. The latter refers to 'the condition of persons whose deafness occurred at an age following the spontaneous acquisition of speech and language'.

The terms '*deafened*' or '*adventitiously deaf*' are sometimes used to describe a person with normal or near normal hearing who, through such causes as disease, drugs, accident or exposure to loud noise, has acquired a profound or total hearing loss. Where the loss has occurred suddenly, the term '*traumatically deafened*' is sometimes used.

People who are *hard of hearing* are those in whom the sense of hearing, although defective, is functional with or without a hearing aid.

In 1951 the then Ministry of Health issued a circular (32/51) requiring County and County Borough Councils to keep a register of handicapped persons who applied for help. A further Circular (25/61) required hearing impaired persons to be registered under the three categories of 'Deaf without speech', 'Deaf with speech' and 'Hard of Hearing'. The current definitions applicable to each category are:

Deaf without speech: 'People who, with or without a hearing aid, have no useful hearing and whose speech is unintelligible.' Many prelingually deaf persons object to this definition, but the law requires local authorities to use it.

Deaf with speech: 'People who with or without a hearing aid have no useful hearing, but whose speech is readily intelligible.'

Hard of Hearing: 'People whose hearing is below par, but who, with or without a hearing aid, have some useful hearing.'

The situation of people who are pre-lingually deafened is not included in this book for three reasons:

First, their problems are different from those of the deafened and hard of hearing. As implied by Ministry of Health definitions, the life-long disability that a person born without usable hearing has to overcome is that of acquiring adequate speech and language. A child who becomes profoundly deaf at, say, the age of seven, will have acquired speech, vocabulary and language pattern in a natural way by hearing words used in conversation and perceiving their meanings in different contexts. In contrast, the child born deaf will, until instructed by specialist teachers, be limited to gestures and unintelligible sounds. To use a somewhat crude analogy, a pre-lingually deaf child is in a similar position to a person who has to learn a foreign language before commencing any other subject. Research has shown that only a minority of such pupils have, on leaving school, achieved a sufficient mastery of speech and lipreading to enable them to talk easily with hearing people and both profoundly deaf and partially hearing pupils have a preference for manual communication methods. For deaf persons who have either failed to achieve socially adequate speech and lipreading skills or who have abandoned the effort to comprehend and participate in the non-deaf milieu, situations will arise where the use of an interpreter is essential.

Pre-lingually deaf persons are, fortunately, much fewer in number than those who are hard of hearing or deafened.

Statistics of hearing loss are unreliable and can never be regarded as more than estimates. Table 1 was prepared in 1991 by the Royal National Institute for Deaf People (RNID) based on data from the Institute of Hearing Research published over the previous ten years.

As shown in Table 2, the vast majority of people with hearing difficulties are older, hard of hearing people. At least three-quarters of the 7.5 million adults with hearing loss are over 60 years old.

Second, prelingually deaf persons form a relatively small proportion of the estimated 7.5 million people with some loss of hearing. Using the 96+ dBHL criterion for 'profound' deafness the RNID estimates that in Great Britain there are about 25,000 such people of all ages.[1] The number increases to nearer 40,000 if the criterion is shifted to 90 dBHL. The British Deaf Association (BDA)

---

1   Any hearing loss in excess of this in the better ear is regarded as 'profound deafness'.

Table 1

Estimates of number of adults in Britain (England, Wales and Scotland) in different hearing categories

Description of Hearing Loss (British Society of Audiology Categories)	dBHL better ear average*	Number of adults (average)	% of total adult population (approx)
Mild hearing loss	25 – 40	5 million	11.33%
Moderate hearing loss	41 – 70	2.2 million	4.99%
Severe hearing loss	71 – 95	0.24 million	0.54%
Profound hearing loss	964	0.06 million	0.14%
	Total	**7.5 million**	**17%**

* db = Decibels   HL = Hearing level.

Minimum intensity at which a subject can hear at a specific frequency in relation to a basic value (6.db) which represents minimum hearing in a normal hearing subjects used in conventional pure tone audiometres. D. Ballantyne *Handbook of Audiological Techniques*. Butterworth-Heinemann 1990, p.201.

The 'average' is across a number of frequencies in the 'better ear'.

Table 2

Estimated incidence of hearing loss irrespective of degree of severity in various age groups of the adult population in Britain (RNID)

Age Group	% with hearing loss
17 – 30 yrs	1.8
31 – 40 yrs	2.8
41 – 50 yrs	8.2
51 – 60 yrs	18.9

estimates that there are about 50,000 people who would say they are part of the 'Deaf Community'. The Deaf community is bound together by the shared experience of being deaf since childhood, the use of a common language and a common culture.

The common language, British Sign Language (BSL) is visual and gestural rather than spoken and is referred to again in Chapter 8. Research has confirmed that BSL is a true language with its own system of grammar and syntax. The BDA has rightly stated that:

> 'As Deaf people recognise the status of their own language, so they have begun to use it with pride. Instead of seeing themselves as "disabled", Deaf people have started to view themselves as part of a linguistic minority in this country.
>
> A great moment for Deaf people was in July 1988 with the unanimous vote of the European Parliament which called on all member states to recognise their own sign language as official, indigenous minority languages of those countries.' (BDA, undated)

The common culture is based internationally and nationally on the World Federation of the Deaf and the BDA and through such organisations as the British Deaf Sports Council and the Deaf Broadcasting Council. At the local level it is focused on deaf clubs or societies provided under the auspices of local authorities or voluntary societies serving local authorities on an agency basis. Within such organizations it is the deaf members who are 'normal' and hearing people who are the 'abnormals'.

Third, the psychological adjustment to loss of hearing is different in the case of those who are deafened than for those who have been born deaf. This different was described in an essay written in 1945 by J D Evans who, at the time, was known as 'The MP for the Deaf':

> 'Between the psychological attitudes of the deaf and the deafened (or hard of hearing) there is an almost unbridgeable gulf. It must be emphasised that at the beginning of their lives the deaf are abnormals shut off from the stream of verbally conveyed ideas which moulds the individual mind to general sameness with the mental pattern of society and throughout their lives the deaf are abnormals struggling towards full normalcy. The deafened on the other hand are normals threatened with all the horror or abnormalcy. To the change in their state and particularly the change in the behaviour of other people towards them they are particularly sensitive ... they will not class themselves with the "true deaf" nor will they approach deaf organisations for help. They are thus a class apart.' ('Voluntary Organisations for the Welfare of the Deaf in *Voluntary Social Services – Their Place in the Modern State*, Methuen.)

This book is written in an attempt to enable hard of hearing and deafened people to understand the nature of acquired hearing loss and, through understanding, adjust positively and constructively.

1

The Mechanism of Hearing

Impaired hearing concentrates the mind wonderfully on the ears, which otherwise we all take for granted. Because the ability to hear well is accepted as normal, most people have only a vague idea of the complex mechanism by which the ear performs its functions of collecting, modifying, amplifying and analyzing sound. Some knowledge of this mechanism is essential, however, to understand the various forms of hearing impairment.

The ear has three parts: the outer, middle and inner ears. The contribution to hearing of each of these parts will be considered, with reference to Figure 1.1.

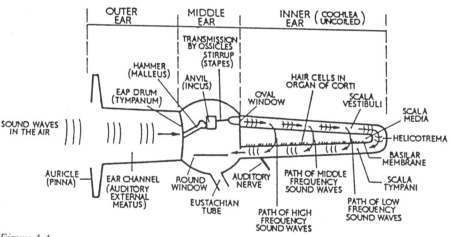

Figure 1.1

The Outer Ear

The outer ear comprises a sound receptor, known as the auricle or pinna, and an inner passage called the ear canal or the external auditory meatus. The auricle resembles a cupped hand and helps to amplify sound waves in front of the ear. When people place a hand behind an ear and cup the ear in the direction of a sound they are, in effect, providing an enlargement of the auricle and thus gaining further amplification – most people will have found themselves doing this in noisy situations.

The external meatus is a cul-de-sac, approximately 25 mm in length, which terminates at the ear drum or tympanum. The tympanum itself is a translucent cone-shaped membrane, about 10 mm in diameter and of approximately the same thickness as a sheet of newspaper. Middle 'C' on a piano, which is a pure tone, causes the tympanum to make 256 vibrations per second – through a distance equivalent only to the diameter of a hydrogen atom (0.000000001 mm).

The Middle Ear

Although the cavity between the inner side of the tympanum and the inner ear is very small, within this space three functions essential to the transmission of sound take place. First, for a reason that will be explained later, vibrations on the tympanum are carried at increased force to the inner ear by means of a lever system consisting of three bones called the ossicles. In order of operation, the ossicles are the malleus, or hammer, which is attached to the tympanum; the incus, or anvil, and the stapes, or stirrup. The bottom part of the stirrup, known as the footplate, fits into a aperture in the inner ear termed the oval window. To give some idea of the minute size of the ossicles, the stapes, the smallest of the three bones, is only about 3 mm high and weighs scarcely 3 milligrams.

The middle ear also maintains an equal air pressure on each side of the tympanum. This pressure is maintained by air which reaches the middle ear through the Eustachian tube. This tube leads into the middle ear from the back of the throat, and can be opened by yawning or swallowing.

Also, the middle ear contains two important muscles, one attached to the tympanum, appropriately called the tensor tympani, and one connected to the stapes called the stapedius. The stapedius has the distinction of being the smallest muscle in the human body. The purpose of these muscles is to give the tympanum and the stapes an opportunity to brace themselves against very loud, low-pitched sounds and thus protect the delicate membrane in the oval window from possible rupture.

The Inner Ear

The inner ear is responsible for the analysis of complex sound frequencies, the transduction of sound waves into nerve impulses and their subsequent transmission to the areas of the brain where they are heard as sounds. The inner ear also contains the three semi-circular canals which play no part in hearing but, together with two small sac-like chambers, the utricle and the saccule, jointly known as the vestibule, are concerned with the maintenance of balance.

The organ of hearing itself is the cochlea (the Greek word for snail, as its external appearance is very similar to the shell of a small snail). If uncoiled the two turns of the shell would form a tube about 30–35 mm long and about 5 mm in diameter. Throughout its length the cochlea is divided into two galleries, partly by a boney shelf and partly by a membrane called the basilar membrane, which varies in thickness from less than 0.001 mm near its basal end to 0.005 mm at the apex of the cochlea. These two galleries are filled with a watery fluid called perilymph. The larger end of the upper gallery, or scala vestibuli, connects with the middle ear at the oval window, where the footplate of the stapes makes a fluid-proof seal. The lower gallery, or scala tympani, meets the middle ear at another aperture, named the round window. The two galleries communicate with each other at the apex through a gap, termed the helicotrema.

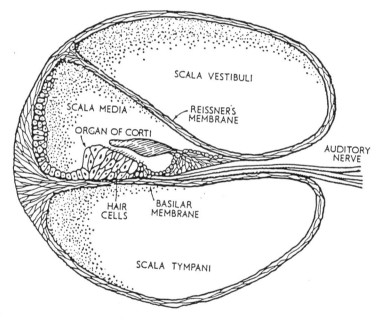

Figure 1.2

From the roof of the upper gallery, another membrane, Reissner's membrane (see Figure 1.2) slopes downwards to form an inner passage shaped like a right-angled triangle, referred to as the scala media. The scala media is also filled with a fluid, endolymph. Resting on the part of the basilar membrane that forms the flow of the scala media is the organ of Corti, named after Alfrenso Corti, who first discovered it in 1851. It is in the organ of Corti that the conversation of sound waves into electrical impulses takes place. Within the organ of Corti are about 23,000 hair cells, arranged in an inner row and four outer rows of rods or pillars. Near the bases of the hair cells are auditory nerve fibres – between 25,000 and 30,000 in number. Although there is just over one nerve fibre to each hair cell the relationship is not on a one-to-one basis and a nerve fibre may act like a telephone party-line in supplying endings to many hair cells. The upper ends of the hair cells pass through a thin membrane called the reticula lamina, and are embedded in a thicker covering membrane which lies like a flap over the organ of corti.

On leaving the cochlea these fibres twist together, rather like the strands of a rope, to form the auditory nerve which conveys the electrical impulses to the temporal portion of the brain.

How the Mechanism Works

Having described the physiology of the ear we can now put the three parts together to see how the mechanism works. Sound waves, which in the young adult vary in frequency from 20 to 20,000 cycles per second or hertz, are collected by the auricle and cause the tympanum to vibrate. These vibrations are conducted across the middle ear by the ossicles; they are then transmitted to the cochlea in the inner ear through the rocking of the stapes in the oval window. So far the sound waves have been transmitted through air; at the oval window they pass into fluid. As a liquid provides higher impedance than air, it follows that the sound pressure on the almost incompressible watery fluid, the perilymph, of the inner ear must be greater than in the highly compressible air of the middle ear. This increased pressure is partly provided by the lever action of the ossicles and partly by the fact that the diameter of the tympanum is about twenty times that of the footplate of the stapes, which therefore exerts twenty times the original pressure on the oval window. The action of the stapes on the oval window causes the perilymph to move over Reissner's membrane round the gap, the helicotrema, and then over the other surface of the basal membrane until it reaches the round window, which thus absorbs the pressure and acts as a kind of safety valve.

A vibration of a particular frequency results in a wave-like ripple which reaches its maximum at a given point along the basilar membrane. Thus, high-frequency sounds cause vibrations near the oval window, while low-frequency ones cause oscillations further along the whole membrane. The movement of the basilar membrane results in a shearing effect between the hair cells of the organ of Corti and the covering (tectorial) membrane; this, in some way not yet understood, causes an electro-chemical reaction in the nerve fibres. The reaction is transmitted by the auditory nerve to the brain. In the brain the information received is decoded and presented as intelligible sound. It has been estimated that the human ear can identify some 350,000 distinct sounds.

The minuteness of the whole apparatus is impressive. So is its high level of perfection. It has been said that the ossicles of the middle ear form a mathematically perfect transmission system, while the contra-actions of the oval and round windows on the perilymph provide an ideal hydraulic system. Finally, although it has taken several pages to describe, the whole process, from the reception of sound waves by the auricle to their interpretation in the auditory cortex of the brain, takes no longer than three-hundredths of a second.

Hearing with Both Ears

Binaural hearing is the term used to describe hearing with two ears; in monaural hearing only one ear is used. Following accident or disease many people have varying degrees of impairment affecting one ear only. Where the 'good' ear is normal or nearly so they may not be greatly inconvenienced.

Binaural hearing provides a spatial dimension to the perception of sound and also enhances clarity. The cues used to localize a sound source are the exact time and intensity at which tones arrive at the two ears. Sounds arrive first at the ear closest to the source and with greater intensity. The head tends to cast an acoustic shadow between the source and the ear on the opposite side to which it is received. The direction of a sound which stimulates both ears can be judged fairly accurately except when it is exactly behind, above or in front of the hearer.

Binaural hearing also enhances our ability to detect and discriminate sounds. Tones heard with both ears sound louder than when heard with one. With two ears sounds at intensities above the threshold are perceived at about 6dB louder than by one ear alone. This is known as the suprathreshold factor. Frequency discrimination is also better with binaural hearing, especially for sounds with very low or very high frequencies. Several researchers have also observed that while the right ear is more efficient at processing speech sounds, the left ear is better with non-speech stimuli such as music.

Coping with the Emotional Effects

It is easier to write about the effects of hearing impairment on personality and behaviour, and their causes, than to suggest just how they may be avoided or overcome. Your adjustment, or your friend's or relative's adjustment, to loss of hearing depends not only on the cause, severity and expected progress of the disability, but also on such variables as age, intelligence, personality, education and support received from family, friends and employers. In making suggestions as to how to cope, it is impossible to avoid generalizations. There is also the danger that a reader, facing the harsh reality of impaired hearing, may dismiss such generalizations as platitudinous preaching. What follows, however, is based not on idle theorizing but on some twenty years' personal experience of hearing impairment. This experience led to the conclusion that if one is to modify the emotional and behavioural effects of hearing loss it is necessary to cultivate at least five virtues: knowledge, honesty, empathy, activity and courage.

Knowledge

The fact that one's ears are dull is no reason why one's mind should not be active. A hearing-impaired person should try to discover, through reading and conversation with others, as much as possible about his or her disability and the procedures, devices and agencies that may exist for its relief. At the simplest level such information will make him or her aware of such gadgets as the flashing door bells and other devices mentioned in Chapter 7. Knowledge about the possible results of hearing loss on behaviour can also prevent some embarrassing situations. For example, people with a conductive loss tend to speak softly; those with a sensorineural loss are prone to shout. Knowing this simple fact will enable a person to modulate his voice appropriately. Being aware that 'substitute aggression' is a negative response to frustration may help an individual to curb any tendency to relieve his tension by venting his frustrations on others. Knowledge enables a person with disabilities to evaluate information and an informed person is much less likely to be taken in by charlatans offering wonder-cures. The very fact that you are reading this page indicates a desire to know something about hearing impairment. This attitude of curiosity and desire for understanding should be maintained.

2
Some Causes of Hearing Loss

Anyone trying to help a person with impaired hearing must have accurate information about the type of loss and how it has arisen. How an otologist may seek such information will be described in Chapter 4. Some of the ways in which the severity and extent of the loss can be measured are outlined in Chapters 3 and 4. This chapter aims to describe the different types of hearing impairment and some of the more common causes.

The Nature of Hearing Loss

A loss of hearing may be placed in one of three categories. *Conductive loss* arises through some cause in the outer ear or the middle ear. *Sensorineural loss* arises in the inner ear and beyond. The term 'sensorineural loss' is now preferred to 'perceptive loss' since it emphasizes that the impairment may be sensory, arising in the cochlea, or neural, affecting the nerve pathways to the brain. Hearing loss may also be *mixed*, owing to abnormalities affecting both the conductive and sensorineural mechanisms.

Apart from the tests described in Chapters 3 and 4 it is possible to make a rough assessment of whether an individual has a predominantly conductive or sensorineural loss by noting the following signs.

	Conductive Loss	Sensorineural Loss
Typical Speech	Low and soft, as the person can hear his or her own voice through bone conduction	Speech is loud with a tendency to shout, as the person has difficultly in hearing his own voice
Toleration of Loudness	Loud sounds and speech can be tolerated	Loud sounds and speech, of an intensity considerably above the threshold of hearing, may cause discomfort.
Background Noise	Hearing is better in a noise in an noise	Noise may adversely affect discrimination, due to recruitment

Both conductive and sensorineural losses can be due to a wide variety of causes, some of which are set out below.

Some Causes of Acquired Hearing Loss

Conductive Loss

(1) Obstructions in the outer ear, due to excessive wax or foreign bodies.

(2) Accidents – these include the rupture of the ear drum by a blow of explosion causing sudden excessive pressure in the outer ear. The ear drum may also be perforated by careless syringing or probing.

(3) Infections – acute or chronic inflammation of the skin lining the outer or middle ear (known respectively as otitis externa and otitis media) can develop from a number of causes. Otitis externa is due to bacterial infections and is sometimes called 'swimmer's ear' as it frequently occurs in swimmers who have had water trapped in their ears. Otitis media, as described later, is closely related to the eustachian tube and can develop from colds, measles, tonsillitis and other infections of the nose and throat.

(4) Otosclerosis is the immobilization of the stapes by a growth of spongy bone.

Sensorineural Loss

(1) Accidents involving head injuries may damage the cochlea. Middle ear surgery is also not without risk.

(2) Virus or bacterial infections (the most common of which are mumps and measles (rubella)) may cause unilateral or bilateral hearing loss. Bacterial meningitis, either meningococcal or tubercular, damaging the cochlea or auditory nerve can cause severe or total loss of hearing which sometimes occurs several months after the onset of the meningitis.

(3) Noise; sudden or prolonged exposure to high intensity sound.

(4) Ototoxic loss can be caused by ear poisoning drugs especially quinine, and antibiotics such as streptomycin, neomycin and Kanamycin.

(5) Presbyacusis or hearing loss associated with old age.

(6) Méniére's disease, which is a triad of symptoms – vertigo, tinnitus and hearing loss.

(7) Miscellaneous causes, including interruption of the blood supply of the inner ear, virus infection of unknown origin or tumours.

Five of the most common causes of hearing loss are discussed here: two being conductive and three of the sensorineural type. A brief reference is also made to tinnitus or head noises which many people with hearing impairment find to be particularly troublesome.

Conductive Loss

Most causes of conductive hearing impairment are due either to inflammation of the middle ear (otitis media) or to a condition known as otosclerosis.

Otitis Media

Otitis media is a general term applied to a variety of infections of the middle ear. In its acute forms otitis media may be due to bacteria spreading up the eustachian tube as a complication of colds, tonsillitis and similar affections of the nose and throat. It may also result from the eustachian tube not working properly, possibly due to infection.

In the case of infection, invading germs cause the mucous membrane lining the middle ear to become inflamed. The inflammation causes fluid secreted in the mucous membrane to exude. If not quickly relieved by antibiotics the pressure exerted by the fluid may lead to rupturing of the ear drum, pain and an ear discharge. Whether the ear drum ruptures or not it will distend and loss of hearing will result.

In the second cause the eustachian tube may not function properly for a number of reasons. If the lining of the eustachian tube becomes swollen due to a cold, or if it is blocked at its entrance by an enlarged adenoid, the tube is unable to perform its function of ensuring that the air pressure on the inside of the drum is equal to that on the outside. The drum is therefore forced inwards and the amount of air remaining in the middle ear is gradually absorbed by the mucous membrane and replaced as fluid. Again, loss of hearing results from the reduced ability of the drum and the ossicles to transmit vibrations.

If promptly treated with sulphonamide drugs and antibiotics such as penicillin there is little danger of permanent hearing impairment resulting from acute otitis media.

There is, however, still the possibility that repeated attacks of acute otitis media may give rise to a chronic condition. Chronic otitis media may be suppurative or non-suppurative. One example of a non-discharging condition is *chronic secretory otitis media* which can occur after an inflammatory infection has been treated by antibiotics. The action of the drugs neutralizes the infection but the fluid, now sterile, remains in the middle ear and gradually thickens until it becomes glue like in consistency. The thicker the 'glue' the more the movement of the three small bones is impeded. If untreated the hearing may deteriorate further because of adhesions on the ossicles or the disruption or destruction of the ossicular chain. Glue ear is very common in children. It has been estimated that most children suffer at least one episode of glue ear before they reach the age of six. About 10 per cent of children suffer prolonged problems and require treatment.

Chronic suppurative otitis media

This may occur when a perforation in the ear drum has become permanent, thereby providing an alternative to the eustachian tube as a route by which infections may enter the middle ear. It is for this reason that anyone with a perforated ear drum is generally advised not to swim. The fluid discharged through the perforation may be either clear and odourless or foul smelling. The distinction is important for while otologists regard the former as relatively harmless the bloody, evil smelling discharge of the latter may be symptomatic of a potentially serious condition known as *cholesteatoma* of the middle ear. A cholesteatoma or cyst contains bone-eroding matter which may destroy the ossicles. If untreated the cyst grows insidiously and may invade the inner ear, thus changing a treatable conductive impairment into an irreversible sensorineural loss and it can also represent a threat to life.

Otosclerosis

Otosclerosis, a disease of the bony wall of the labyrinth, is the commonest cause of hearing impairment during the period from young adulthood up to early middle age. The term otosclerosis, meaning a hardening of the ear bone, is misleading since the effect of the disease is to replace the normal hard bone with soft spongy bone. Otosclerosis has been called a 'pathological enigma'; as yet, in spite of much research, no firm conclusions on its cause have been reached.

Otosclerosis develops insidiously and may be noticed by people in their late teens or early twenties although the peak incidence occurs at about thirty years of age. The hearing loss is due to the stapes becoming fixed, or anchylosed, in the oval window because of an overgrowth of the spongy bone. At first the impairment may be slight although hearing acuity deteriorates at varying rates (there may even be periods when the loss gets no worse). In its later stages the disease may invade the inner ear so that the condition changes from a conductive to a mixed loss.

Otosclerosis of course shows the general indictions of conductive impairment described earlier in this chapter. It also has the following characteristics:

- It is estimated to be twice as prevalent in women as in men; pregnancy may be a precipitating factor.
- There is usually, although not necessarily, a family history of 'deafness'.

- With conductive otosclerosis, bone conduction will be better than air conduction; it may be possible to hear on the telephone even when there is difficulty in hearing normal speech.

- Tinnitus is often present and in mild cases may be the most distressing symptom.

- The hearing loss usually begins in one ear and then in most cases becomes bilateral; but the degree of hearing loss is not the same in both ears.

- Otosclerosis is more prevalent in white than in black races, and among the fair-haired.

While otitis media and otosclerosis are the two most important causes of conductive impairment they are dissimilar in several respects. Otitis media is a disease of childhood, although its consequences may persist through adult life. Otosclerosis becomes apparent in early adulthood. The hereditary 'deafness' that can often be traced in otosclerosis patients does not arise in otitis media. There are also differences that can be detected only by the otologist; in otitis media both the ear drum and the eustachian tube show signs of abnormality; in otosclerosis they are usually normal.

Sensorineural Hearing Loss

Although sensorineural loss may occur at any stage of life it is particularly associated with birth and the degenerative consequences of ageing. Congenital impairment is beyond the scope of this book but the causes of profound hearing loss at or before birth include viral infections such as rubella or German measles contracted by the mother during the first three months of pregnancy; Kernicterus or nuclear jaundice which results when a mother lacking the Rhesus Factor (antigen) conceives a Rhesus positive baby, and anoxia or lack of oxygen, causing brain damage at the time of birth.

The birth of babies with a hearing loss caused by congenital rubella can be predicted by good ante-natal screening and inoculation.

A useful distinction can also be made between *congenital* and *hereditary* hearing loss. The former implies that hearing loss was present at birth and may include acquired as well as hereditary factors. Hereditary loss applies to those cases where the causes were present in the fertilised ovum and transmitted as a dominant or recessive characteristic. Where one parent carries a dominant deaf gene the risk of a hearing impaired baby is as high as 50 per cent. In the recessive form in which both parents must be carriers of a hearing characteristic that produces sensorineural impairment the risk is about 25 per cent.

In this chapter we shall consider three manifestations of sensorineural impairment: Méniére's disease, noise induced loss and presbyacusis or hearing loss as an accompaniment of growing older.

Méniére's Disease

Méniére's Disease is named after Prosper Méniére, a Paris physician who, in a paper presented to the Paris Academy of Medicine in 1861, drew attention to the inner ear as the source of the diverse symptoms that comprise the condition which he described as follows:

> 'A young healthy man experiences, for no apparent reason, vertigo, nausea and vomiting, an inexpressibly distressing state takes all his strength away, his pale face bathed with sweat suggests he is about to faint. Often the patient, after feeling unsteady, falls dazed to the ground without being able to get up and lying on his back is unable to open his eyes without seeing surrounding objects spinning around him. The slightest movement of his head makes the vertigo and nausea worse and the vomiting starts again as soon as the patient tries to change position. Incidents of the same kind recurred frequently causing serious anxiety especially as between each crisis he was inclined to vertigo and deafness. The patient could not move his head suddenly, turn to right or left without losing his balance; his gait became unsteady, he veered involuntarily to one side and the ground appeared uneven — sudden movements resulted in functional disorders of this kind. If the patient when he was lying down moved suddenly into a horizontal position, immediately the bed and all the surrounding objects began spinning, he felt as if he was on a ship on the high seas and became nauseated. If he got up suddenly into a vertical position exactly the same phenomena occurred and if he tried to walk he would immediately fall down ...

> The patient continued to complain of other symptoms. For example, noises in his ears, often very loud and very persistent, and a noticeable hearing loss on one side and sometimes even on both sides and it was because of this that a doctor specialising in ear disease was called in. I examined the organs and did not discover the slightest trade of a lesion but I noted the relation between the deafness and the 'cerebral troubles'. I have frequently seen similar cases and I became interested in researching them further. I came to the conclusion that the cerebral and auditory lesions were a single illness.'

Méniére's patient exhibited the three symptoms that characterize this disorder: intermittent attacks of vertigo accompanied by tinnitus and hearing loss.

Three stages of the disease have been identified by the American Academy of Ophthalmology and Otolaryngology. Initially, episodes of vertigo are associated with reversible fluctuating low frequency hearing loss. This stage is superseded by one in which there is an established but still fluctuating hearing loss together with episodes of vertigo. Finally the hearing loss ceases to be fluctuating and is constant, accompanied at intervals by attacks of vertigo. Usually the vertigo attacks are preceded and attended by an increase in tinnitus or feeling of pressure in the ear.

Ménière's disease, which affects about one in every thousand of the population, usually begins between the ages of 30 and 50 years. The condition rarely starts in old age. Although initially affecting only one ear, Ménière's disease becomes bilateral in about 50 per cent of cases. The earlier the onset of the trouble the greater the probability that both ears will be affected.

During the remission intervals, most people can continue with their normal occupations and activities. The Ménière's Society, however, has published a useful leaflet *Ménière's Disease, Driving and the Law*. This points out that although there are no clearly defined laws relating to Ménière's disease, if one suffers from 'sudden disabling attacks of vertigo' then that person may not legally drive. Under Section 5 of the Road Traffic Act it is also an offence to drive while under the influence of drugs. Except for *Serc* this includes some of the drugs used for Ménière's disease treatment. Therefore if you drive and have been diagnosed as having Ménière's disease you must notify both your Insurance Company and the DVLC. Should you fail to do so and then have an accident you could be charged with failure to notify your insurer and the DVLC and unless able to prove that you did not have an attack prior to the event you might also be held responsible for an accident, even if it was not your fault. Working on ladders should also be avoided.

A somewhat intimidating name for Ménière's disease is endolymphatic hydrops. This name derives from the fact that we now know that the symptoms are caused by a surplus of endolymphatic fluid in the inner ear. This surplus apparently increases the pressure in the scala media, causing a deterioration in the hair cells. This pressure concurrently overstimulates the semi-circular canals on which our sense of balance depends, thereby producing the sensation of dizziness. The cause of the increased endolymphatic pressure has not been conclusively established.

Accurate diagnosis is essential, since vertigo is not confined to Ménière's disease. Other ear conditions in which dizziness is a symptom may be harder to treat. Such conditions include labyrinthitis and disorders of the acoustic nerve.

Reference to the treatment of Ménière's disease is made in Chapter 4. In passing, however, it is useful to remember that the intervals between attacks make it difficult for an otologist to be sure whether an apparent improvement is due to the prescribed treatment or to natural causes.

Presbyacusis

Some degree of hearing loss is one of the burdens of growing older. Of course not all elderly people are sufficiently hard of hearing to have difficulty in social situations. In every decade of life after 20, however, there is an increase in the proportion of those of us who are conscious of some deterioration in the acuity of our hearing. It has been estimated that about 25 per cent of 65-year-olds have more difficulty in hearing than they did at 30. At 70 and 80 the percentages increase to 33.3 and 50 per cent respectively.

Presbyacusis, or 'senile deafness' is characterized by an increasing loss in the higher-frequency range. It becomes difficult to hear speech clearly; an elderly person will complain that 'people won't speak up'. When they do, recruitment or increased sensitivity to sound will cause them to complain that 'there's no need to shout'. Recruitment also intensifies the difficulty of hearing in group situations where there is background noise.

There are various reasons why our hearing deteriorates in later life. Nobel prize winner George Von Békésy points out that 'the ageing of the ear is not difficult to understand if we assume that the elasticity of the tissues in the inner ear declines in the same way as that of the skin. It is well known that the skin becomes less resilient as we grow old – something that you can easily test by lifting the skin on the back of your hand and measuring the time it takes to fall back. This degeneration of inner ear tissue begins at the basal end of the cochlea and is accompanied by atrophic changes in the auditory nerve fibres. One researcher, Meyer zum Gottesberge has compared this effect to the wear on a stair carpet. The carpet represents the hair cells and their connected neurons. People climbing the 'stairs' represent the vibrations at different frequencies in the inner ear. The low frequencies move over the entire carpet, wearing it evenly, but the high frequencies use only the first flight of 'stairs'. Consequently, the wear on the carpet decreases from the entrance as one goes towards the top of the spiral. As time passes, the parts of this delicate apparatus activated by the higher frequencies are those that receive the most wear and therefore are the first to show the effects of prolonged exposure to noise.

An interesting problem is why presbyacusis is more pronounced in some people than others. It seems that the rate of degeneration may be influenced by the lifetime experience of the ear in respect of its exposure to noise.

Samuel Rosen, an American Otologist, who is referred to later in this book, studied the Maabaans, a primitive African tribe living in an environment where the noise levels only occasionally exceeded 40 db, indicated that a male Maabaan aged between 70 and 79 had keener hearing than a sample of Americans in the 30–39 age range who had been exposed to the noises of modern civilization.[1]

An alternative hypothesis is that the absence of stressful living rather than merely noise could be an important factor. Noise, of course, may be a factor in stress. One reason why women tend to experience hearing loss in age less frequently than men may be that, in general, they are often less exposed to noisy conditions. It is also known that blood pressure and local atherosclerosis (hardening and thickening of the small arteries) may be connected with a limited hearing loss.

Rosen also attempted to show that a diet with a high fat content may lead not only to cardiovascular disease but to inferior hearing in later life.

The apparent difference in the hearing ability of individuals of a given age may even be due to psychological factors. The author recalls reading about an old gentleman who, after listening to a garrulous wife for almost fifty years, had heard enough and was happy to withdraw into the quiet world provided by impaired hearing.

Tinnitus

Tinnitus, the Latin word for 'ringing' or 'jingling' may be defined as a subjective experience of noise when there is no external stimulation. Head noises accompany almost all forms of hearing impairment and manifest themselves in a wide variety of ways. A somewhat pedantic distinction is occasionally made between tinnitus and 'auditory hallucination'. In tinnitus the sounds are heard as simple monotones, variously described as 'buzzing', 'ringing', 'throbbing' and so forth. In auditory hallucination, more complex and cacophonous sounds are experienced so that the person concerned may complain of 'guns going off in his head' or 'a devil's orchestra'. One unfortunate lady stated that her tinnitus sounded like 'the first three bars of God Save the Queen endlessly repeated'. Many people find tinnitus more distressing than hearing loss, but to get the matter in perspective about 85 per cent of those who experience tinnitus do find it intrusive.

Causes of Tinnitus

The causes of tinnitus are as diverse as those of hearing loss and possibly even more numerous. The most common causes may be classified under four headings: obstructions to sound conduction, pathological alterations in the cells of the

---

1   Rosen. S. (1973) *None so Deaf – the Autobiography of Dr. Samuel Rosen.* W.H. Allen and Co Ltd, pp.204–213.

cochlea sensory system, physical distortion of the cochlea sensory system and a number of miscellaneous reasons.

OBSTRUCTIONS TO SOUND CONDUCTION

Such obstructions occur in our outer and middle ears and include:

- Wax in the outer ear
- Perforated eardrum
- Otitis media – in which fluid in the middle ear results in crackling or bubbling head noises
- Otosclerosis.

PATHOLOGICAL CHANGES IN THE COCHLEA CELLS

This may be due to:

- Presbyacusis
- Acoustic Trauma – resulting from blast or noise
- Toxic Labrynthitis – caused by drugs including aspirin, quinine and antibiotics especially those of the 'mycin' family, e.g. Streptomycin, Neomycin, Viomycin.

PHYSICAL DISTORTION OF THE COCHLEA SYSTEM

This is usually responsible for the tinnitus that accompanies Méniére's disease.

OTHER CAUSES

These include concussion, areo-otitis caused by air pressure changes when flying and tinnitus resulting from other conditions, giving rise to high blood pressure or changes due to Paget's Disease.

Tinnitus may be confined to one ear, when it is indicative of a local cause or may be bilateral, which is symptomatic of a general condition. There is also a third type, central tinnitus, when the noises seem to be diffused all over the head rather than located specifically. Only rarely is central tinnitus due to an ear condition.

The relief of tinnitus

What an otologist can do to relieve tinnitus is discussed in Chapter 4. There are, however, a number of DIY measures that may be helpful. These include diet, herbs, relaxation, keeping occupied and joining a tinnitus help group.

DIET

Diet is a contributory factor to improved general health rather than specifically related to tinnitus. While there is no conclusive evidence that losing weight will of itself lead to reduced hypertension it is known that slim persons tend to be less hypersensitive than those who are overweight.

Eat plenty of fruit, stick to low fat cheese, avoid junk foods and heavy meals at bedtime. The most important advice, however, is to reduce your intake of salt and give up salt rich foods such as salami, pickles and salted fish. Reduced salt intake, as stated in Chapter 4, is particularly important in relation to Méniére's Disease.

HERBS

Herbal remedies are ineffectual in the treatment of tinnitus caused by damage or degeneration of the hair cells in the cochlea. There is, however, some evidence that the leaves of the Gingko Biloba or Chinese Maidenhair Tree contain ingredients that relieve tinnitus and improve hearing, but whether this is a universal remedy or efficacious only in selected cases is, as yet, unproven. It may be possible to obtain Gingko Biloba in tablet form through a health shop.

Other herbs which it is claimed are beneficial in reducing tinnitus include garlic, ginger, hops and yeast. How these work is uncertain. Garlic, obtainable in odourless capsules, is a mild antibiotic and may build up the body-s resistance to colds and minor infections. Yeast is a nerve nutrient. It is likely that such herbs reduce tinnitus by improving one's general health.

DRUG AVOIDANCE

The side-effects of some drugs may cause or exacerbate tinnitus. Such drugs include alcohol, aspirin, caffeine, cortisone, quinine and some tranquillisers.

Alcohol is ambivalent in its effects. In moderation it may have a beneficial relaxing effect. Conversely, too much alcohol by increasing blood flow may aggravate tinnitus. You should avoid heavy drinking.

Aspirin is an analgesic drug (painkiller) used to treat disorders such as headache and toothache. It does, however, increase tinnitus due to the fact that it irritates rather than calms the acoustic nerve. People with tinnitus are therefore advised to use alternative painkillers such as paracetamol. Unfortunately, aspirin is an ingredient used in most anti-inflammatory drugs used for the relief of arthritis. In consequence arthritics are susceptible to tinnitus.

Caffeine is a stimulant drug found in coffee beans and tea leaves. Drinking an excessive amount of coffee might increase the tinnitus you already have: cutting down your coffee intake will probably reduce your tinnitus.

Cortisone is used among other things to reduce inflammation in severe allergic rheumatic and connective diseases. One unfortunate side-effect is that, like salt, it can increase tinnitus by altering the level of your body fluids.

Quinine is the oldest drug treatment for malaria. There is, however, a high risk of hearing loss, tinnitus and other side-effects such as headache, nausea and blurred vision. Tonic water contains quinine and should be avoided.

Tranquillisers including Dilatin and Valium tend to aggravate tinnitus.

RELAXATION

Tinnitus is stressful. Your tinnitus may make you more anxious or frustrated or even interfere with work and sleep. The stress is enhanced because it is impossible adequately to describe to others what you are experiencing.

Therefore a vicious circle is set up.

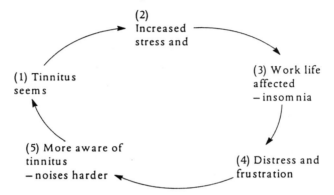

It follows that anything that can reduce stress is likely to make you less aware of the tinnitus. One way of counteracting stressfulness is by relaxation. As a booklet *Helpful Hints* published by the Sheffield Tinnitus Association puts it:

- The more relaxed the body, the more relaxed the mind
- The more relaxed the body, the easier the symptoms get
- The more relaxed you are, the more you can allow life to come to you without worrying about it
- By learning to relax you can find your way into a state of inner peacefulness
- By learning to relax you can recognize when you are becoming tense and stop this happening.

You can relax in simple ways: taking a break, having a nap, watching the birds. Deep breathing is helpful. Lie full length with your legs slightly apart and your arms at your side while you inhale calmly and deeply, filling your lungs with air and then exhaling while thinking of the word 'relax' will reduce tension. There are also ways in which you can be 'taught' to relax. These include relaxation tapes, biofeedback, hypnotherapy and yoga.

Relaxation tapes obtainable from health shops and music stores play soothing music or speech through a personal stereo and are helpful in breaking the stress of tinnitus. A pillow speaker is obtainable from TANOY stores at low cost. This has a mini-plug which connects to a radio or cassette player to listen to a cassette or radio programme without disturbing others as an alternative to head or earphones which may be uncomfortable in bed. A list of tapes is obtainable from the RNID Tinnitus Helpline.

Biofeedback is information provided by various diagnostic appliances used to monitor bodily functions such as heart-rate, blood pressure, muscle contraction, skin resistance, sweating and brain waves. These responses to stress can register as low amplitude voltages which, when amplified, can be used to energize indicators such as an electric meter needle, a tone of varying pitch or a computer display.

The theory is that since tinnitus is a stress related condition you can, by the use of such indicators, be taught to monitor the stress level resulting from head noises. Later, through conditioning, you will be able to do so without the use of the machine. This self-monitoring, when learned, can help you to relax, which enables a degree of tinnitus once considered unacceptable to be tolerated.

The success of the biofeedback is likely to be greater when the tinnitus can be treated indirectly by controlling a bodily function such as increased blood pressure which gives rise to the condition. Your personality can also significantly influence the benefit received from biofeedback.

There is, however, reliable research evidence relating to the effectiveness of biofeedback in reducing anxiety and tension which enhances tinnitus. If you require further information about biofeedback services you should consult your general practitioner or hearing clinic.

HYPNOTHERAPY

Hypnosis, which is 'a trance-like state of altered awareness characterized by extreme suggestibility' is often used therapeutically, as a means of helping people to relax. While hypnosis should only be administered by a qualified hypnotherapist, it is possible to learn self-hypnosis which usually involves the repeating of certain phrases or imagining relaxing scenes. An account of a small scale trial of hypnosis on 14 tinnitus patients at the ENT Department of Guy's Hospital, London, concluded that while a significant attack on tinnitus by suggestion under hypnosis was unsuccessful there was nevertheless evidence that the common consequence of tinnitus such as irritability and depression could, in some people,

be modified by hypnotherapy. Information regarding hypnotherapists may be
obtained from the British Hypnotherapy Association.

Yoga or Transcendental Meditation is a general term for a number of spiritual
disciplines developed by Hinduism and Buddhism to achieve higher conscious-
ness, liberation from ignorance and suffering, and rebirth. The main form of yoga
practised in the West is hatha yoga which emphasizes physical control and
postures. The concentration on breathing and the alternative stretching and
relaxing designed to affect all parts of the body have been found to have beneficial
effects on health, especially in lowering raised blood pressure. The main application of yoga to tinnitus is as a taught relaxation technique. Yoga tuition
including exercise is widely available through evening classes. Further information can be obtained from the Yoga Centre.

KEEPING BUSY

Relaxation does not necessarily mean doing nothing. As William Cooper
(1731–1800) observed:

> Absence of occupation is not rest;
>
> A mind quite vacant is a mind distressed.

Most people with tinnitus find that the noises re less intrusive when they are
occupied and more troublesome at night when they are less busy. Hobbies that
absorb your attention can make you less conscious of tinnitus. Possible hobbies
are legion, although gardening, handicrafts, painting and writing are among the
most popular. Walking and swimming provide both healthy exercise and a
healthy tiredness that promotes relaxation. Even assembling a jigsaw can be a
source of relaxation therapy.

JOINING A TINNITUS SUPPORT GROUP

The British Tinnitus Association has set up a number of local support groups
of associations. Such groups enable people with tinnitus to meet socially and
exchange information about their common problem. Details of these can be
obtained from the BTA.

3
Measuring Hearing and Hearing Loss

Sound is one of the most important factors in our environment. In the form of speech, it is the most convenient form of communication. It is often a source of pleasure, as when we listen to music. When sound becomes excessive, distracting or even painful, such as the din of machinery in a factory, the blare of an unwanted radio or the scream of a jet engine we have the problem of *noise*. Without sound our world seems empty and dead.

If we know something of the nature of sound and its relationship to hearing, we can understand how our hearing may be measured and how such measurements can be used by an otologist to determine the nature of his patient's loss — and then what assistance he can provide.

Sound and Decibels

The sensation of hearing takes place when a stimulus called a *sound* is detected by the ear. The source of this stimulus can always be traced to the movement or vibration of a body, although this movement may be so minimal or rapid that it cannot be seen. Place your fingers on your throat as you talk or sing and you will be able to feel your windpipe vibrating. Strike a tuning fork on the table and listen for its sound. If you then grasp the prongs you will feel the quivering metal.

Sound reaches the ear in the form of waves that originate at the sound source and travels through the air at about 244 metres per second. A sound wave is characterized by a to-and-fro movement known as compression and expansion. A vibrating body is surrounded by particles of air; as it vibrates the particles are first compressed or pushed outwards so that they collide with neighbouring particles, between the movements the particles spread out and expansion takes place. When a compression arrives at the ear, the slightly higher pressure causes the drum to be pushed inwards. With expansion the pressure behind the drum causes it to bulge outwards.

Sound waves differ according to their complexity but with what is known as a pure tone such as a note on a piano, a sound wave may be pictured as in Figure 3.1.

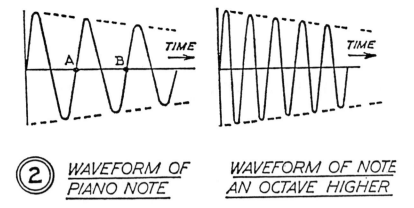

WAVEFORM OF   WAVEFORM OF NOTE
PIANO NOTE   AN OCTAVE HIGHER

Figure 3.1

From the standpoint of this book the most important attributes of a soundwave are its frequency, pitch and intensity.

The *frequency* of a sound wave is the number of cycles of compression and expansion that take place within one second. The note *Middle C* on a piano has 256 cycles per second. One cycle is completed when the line on the diagram has travelled between two corresponding points. On the first graph these points are marked A and B. As can be seen, a note an octave higher would have twice as many vibrations. The term *cycles per second* has now been replaced by the expression Hertz (Hz). This term comes from the name of the German physicist Heinrich R Hertz (1857–94). If, therefore, in one second a sound results in 1500 compressions and expansions, it is said to have a frequency of 1500 Hz. A young adult with normal hearing has an audible range from 15 Hz to about 20,000 Hz.

Within this range the human ear is particularly sensitive to sounds that fall between 1000 and 4000 Hz. Sounds below the audible range are described as infrasonic while those above are referred to as ultrasonic. Some sound frequencies are shown in Figure 3.2.

The *pitch* of a sound is determined by the number of wave vibrations per second or Hz. The greater the length of a wave, the lower will be the number of wavelengths passing a point in one second. Conversely, the shorter the wavelength the higher the pitch. A very low note, say 15 Hz, has a wavelength of about 0.017 metres. The higher the wavelength the higher the pitch. As we grow older, the sensitivity of our ears to higher frequencies and the ability to hear high-pitched tones is progressively reduced.

Intensity is the amount of energy put into a sound by its source; this is shown by the amplitude of the sound wave. The larger the amplitude, that is, the pressure produced by the sound wave, the louder it sounds. Loudness and intensity are different but are related since loudness depends on intensity. If we strike a tuning fork gently, for example, it will produce a soft tone and result in a wave of low amplitude. When the fork is struck more forcefully, the tone will be louder and the amplitude of the wave will be greater. In both cases, however, the frequency of the note will be the same. As we know, sound fades as it travels through the air. As sound waves travel from their source, the amplitude of the compression–expansion is reduced as a function of the distance travelled. In simple terms this means that if you are in the open air listening to a person standing two feet away and he moves to a distance of four feet, his voice will sound not half but only one-quarter as loud as it did before. Every hearing-impaired person should therefore discover the approximate distance at which he can hear a conversation under different conditions, such as in a quiet room or out of doors, and ensure that he keeps within this range of the speaker.

Sound intensity can be measured in two ways, namely in terms of the *energy* given out by a source, for example, the noise made by a jet aircraft taking off, or the variations caused in the normal atmospheric *pressure.* Sound energy and sound pressure are related. As can be seen from Figure 3.2, sound energy increases as the square of sound pressure. Thus a tenfold increase in pressure corresponds with a hundredfold (10 x 10) increase in sound energy. For comparing changes in either energy or pressure we use *decibels.*

Sound	*Frequency (Hz)*
Lowest note on piano	27.5
Lowest note of bass singer	100
Middle C on piano	256
Upper range of soprano	1000
Highest note on piano	4180
Limit of hearing for older persons	12000
Limit of human hearing	16,000–20,000

Figure 3.2. Some Sound Frequencies

There are several reasons why decibels are confusing to people who are not physicists or mathematicians. First, a decibel is not a unit such as a volt or metre, but a ratio. The noise produced by two bees will obviously be twice that of one bee. Similarly, if you listen to one jet aircraft and then to two planes simultane-

Ratio Equivalent Sound Energy (Power) Ratio	Decibel Equivalent	Sound Pressure Ratio
1:1	0	1:1
100:1	10	10:1 (10^1)
10,000:1	20	100:1 (10^2)
1,000,000:1	30	1,000:1 (10^3)
100,000,000:1	40	10,000:1 (10^4)
10,000,000,000:1	50	100,000:1 (10^5)
1,000,000,000,000:1	60	1,000,000:1 (10^6)
100,000,000,000,000:1	70	10,000,000:1 (10^7)

Figure 3.3. Sound Energy and Sound Pressure Units and their Decibel Equivalents

ously, the loudness will also be doubled. Although the noise of the jets will be vastly greater than the bees, the relative increase in sound will be the same in both cases. A given number of decibels therefore expresses the ratio of a measured amount of sound energy or sound pressure to a reference intensity or pressure. In a simplified form a decibel can be expressed as either

$$\frac{\text{sound energy}}{\text{reference sound energy}} \quad \text{or} \quad \frac{\text{sound pressure}}{\text{reference sound pressure}}$$

All measurements must start somewhere. If we measure the height of a mountain, for example, the reference points is sea level. Without such a reference point, statements such as *a sound level of 60 dB* are meaningless because we have no standard of comparison. With sound, therefore, the international reference point is the threshold of hearing which is the quietest, pure tone audible at 1000 Hz to a person with normal hearing. Statements of the form that a sound is 60 dB mean that the sound is 60 dB more intense than the international reference point.

A second source of confusion is that we use different reference points in respect of sound energy and sound pressure. Where sound energy is concerned, power is measured in watts per square metre and the threshold of hearing is taken as $0.000,000,000,001$ watts/m^2 or 10-12/m^2 (10 to the minus 12 watt per square metre). Where sound pressure is used this is expressed in Newtons per square metre (N/m^2) for which the term *pascal* has been internationally agreed. One pascal is about 10-millionths of the normal atmospheric pressure. The threshold of hearing in this case is taken as 20 micro pascals or 0.00002 of a pascal. This latter reference was taken because it is the smallest sound pressure to which the human ear will respond.

A third point of difficulty is that billions and millions are cumbersome numbers. This is, however, a way out. Any number can be expressed in terms of 10 to a given power; e.g. $1000 = 10 \times 10 \times 10$ or 10^3. Originally sound was measured in terms of *Bels*, a unit named after Alexander Graham Bell. One Bel was equal to a tenfold increase in sound energy. Three Bels, therefore, corresponded to 10^3. Using this notation, the awkward number of 1,000,000,000,000 used in Figure 3.3 can be reduced to 12 Bels or 12 tenfold increases. The Bel, however, was too large a unit for electronic engineers who required greater precision and in 1929 the *decibel* (dB) or one 10th of a Bel was universally adopted. A 60 dB difference in the million) times more intense than the other. The decibel equivalents of some everyday sounds are shown in Figure 3.4.

Decibel Equivalent	Relative Intensities (approximate examples)
0	Threshold of hearing
20	Still day in the country away from traffic
40	Rustle of leaves in gentle breeze
60	Normal conversation at distance of 1 metre in quiet room
80	Traffic in busy street
100	Very noisy factory (may damage hearing)
120	Jet aircraft taking off at 150 metres
140	At 140 dB a sound will not be observed as such. The sensitive parts of the ear will be shaken so violently that the sensation will be experienced as pain rather than sound.

Figure 3.4. Decibel Equivalents

Audiometry and Audiometers

The word 'audiometry' is a compound of Latin *audire* (to hear) and Greek *metron* (measure). Audiometry makes use of several types of audiometer according to the particular aspect of hearing to be measured. We can, for example, distinguish screening, diagnostic and clinical audiometers.

Screening audiometers are used for the rapid assessment for hearing against given criteria.

Diagnostic audiometers perform most standard or all standard pure tone and speech tests.

Clinical audiometers enable a comprehensive range of sophisticated tests to be undertaken including Békeséy testing.

Irrespective of their range and operation, however, all audiometers incorporate three essential features: a frequency selector; a hearing level selector; and a receiver, which may either be an earphone or a bone-conduction vibrator.

The frequency selector selects the frequency at which the ear is to be tested. All audiometers test in steps of one octave at frequencies of 125, 250, 500, 1000, 2000, 4000 and 8000 Hz while for clinical work, half octave frequencies of 750, 1500, 3000, and 6000 Hz are also provided.

The hearing level selector presents each frequency at a defined output pressure level, usually from minus 10 dB to 100 dB, which is calibrated to the standard first laid down in 1964 by the International Standards Organisation and incorporated in ISO 8253-2 1992. This standard was based on a hearing survey of a large number of otologically normal people aged 18–30 years. An otoligically normal subject is defined as:

A person in a normal state of health who is free from all signs or symptoms of hearing disease and from obstructing wax in the ear canals and who has no history of undue exposure to noise.

On most audiometers the hearing level selector is divided into steps of 5 dB.

In addition, audiometers are filled with an interrupted switch, a masking device and a speech circuit.

The interrupter switch is used to present or withdraw a signal to the ear. The masking device is used when a person's two ears are markedly dissimilar in sensitivity: if the sound pressure required for audibility in the poorer ear is so high that the better ear picks up the signal indirectly or by bone conduction, the accuracy of the test will be affected. Audiometers can present *white noise* or some other masking sound to the ear that is not being tested. (White noise is defined as *noise whose power spectral density is independent of frequency*. More simply, white noise is a continuous noise, for example the hissing of steam, in which high, middle and low frequencies are equally represented. As the power is distributed uniformly over the whole spectrum it is, by analogy with light called white noise.)

Like the hearing level selector, the masking dial or *noise attenuator* as it is technically called is in steps of 5 dB.

For social adequacy the ability to hear speech is clearly more important than to detect pure tones. The speech circuit provides a means by which lists of words, either on pre-recorded tapes or spoken by the examiner can be presented either through the headphones or bone conduction receiver. Speech audiometry is referred to later in this chapter.

Audiometers are becoming increasingly more sophisticated. An illustration of an audiological suite comprising an advanced clinical audiometer, middle-ear analyzer for tympanometry, printer and VDU is shown in Figure 3.5.

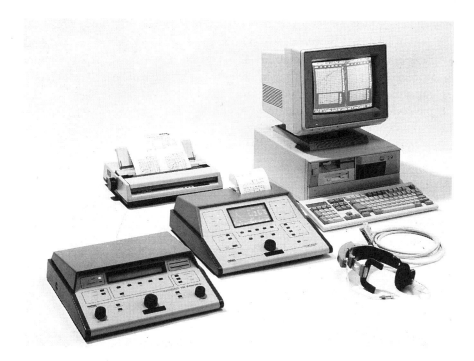

Figure 3.5. Typical Audiological Suite (courtesy P C Werth Ltd)

Computerization can take the routine out of audiometric testing. Using a keyboard the test person's name, identification, age and previous test results can be stored and retrieved from the memory. Results can be viewed visually on the liquid display, graphically on the cathode ray tube monitor and printed out as hard copy. Test results stored in the memory can, by means of the computer interface, be downloaded to an external database.

Audiometric Testing

A routine audiometric test will normally comprise tests of your ability to hear pure tones by air and bone conduction and to hear and understand speech.

Impedance testing provides additional information about the functioning of your middle and inner ears and Eustachian tubes. More sophisticated audiometric tests include Békeséy and Evoked Response tests.

Taking a Pure Tone Test

The purpose of pure tone screening or diagnostic audiometry is to determine your hearing threshold (HTL). Your HTL is the level of sound at which under specified conditions you give 50 per cent correct detection responses on a specified number of trials. More colloquially, it is your ability to just detect pure tones of varying intensities presented at different frequencies. Your ability to hear sounds will be tested by both air and bone conduction.

Air conduction (AC) is your ability to hear sounds in the normal way by which signals received by your ear drum are conducted by the ossicles to the perceiving apparatus in the inner ear and the brain.

Bone conduction (BC) is the transmission of sound energy through the bones of the skull.

Pure tone tests made by an audiometer are charted on an audiogram which shows your threshold of hearing for pure tones at given frequencies. An example

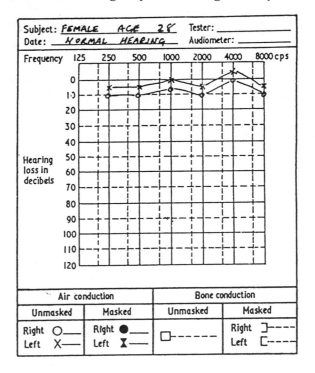

Figure 3.6

of a pure tone audiogram for a person with normal hearing is shown in Figure 3.6.

In the above example, results for both the left and right ears are plotted on the one graph. The British Society of Audiology, however, recommends a separate graph for each ear using the audiogram form and symbols shown in Figure 3.7.

Pure tones are tested very simply. The tester will place a pair of headphones on your head and present you with a signal. You indicate whether you have heard the signal as instructed. Normally, this will be by pressing a button which records the response on the audiometer, by tapping the table, raising your finger, or simply saying *Yes*. After a trial run the Examiner will begin the test. Your response should be for as long as you hear the signal which should last from between one and three seconds.

When the Examiner is satisfied that you *know the drill*, testing can commence.

It is usual for the tester to try your right ear first unless you have indicated a difference between the ears, in which case the test will commence with the better ear. Normally the tester will start by establishing your hearing threshold at 1000 Hz.

There are two approaches to finding the threshold. In what is known as the *descending* method the tester will present a tone which, on the basis of his observations and information so far, he assumes you will be able to hear. Thus, at 1000 Hz the hearing selector may be turned to 40 dB. If you hear this tone, the tester will turn it off with the interrupter switch and turn the selector down by 10 dB intervals until you are no longer able to hear the signal. The selector will then be turned up in 5 dB steps until the signal is again heard. Once again the selector will be turned down in 5 dB intervals until the sound is inaudible. This increasing and decreasing will be continued until you have made three consistent responses. The level of these responses will be taken as you threshold at 1000 Hz.

The *ascending* method is broadly similar, except that, initially, the hearing selector will be set at 1 dB and will be turned up in 5 dB steps until you indicate that you are receiving the signal. Again your responses will be checked until you report three consistent indications of the threshold. After testing at 1000 Hz other frequencies will be taken, usually beginning with the higher levels, i.e. 2000, 4000, 6000, 8000 and then reverting to the lower frequencies. The tester will plot your responses for each ear on the audiogram or audiograms. As can be seen from Figure 3.6, the symbols O and X are used to indicate an air-conduction test for the right and left ears respectively. A red pen or pencil is often used to indicate bone conduction and blue for air conduction.

After air-conduction tests have been completed the headphones will be taken off and a bone-conduction vibrator applied to the mastoid of one ear, unless there

PURE TONE AUDIOGRAM

Name   Age   Date   Case No.

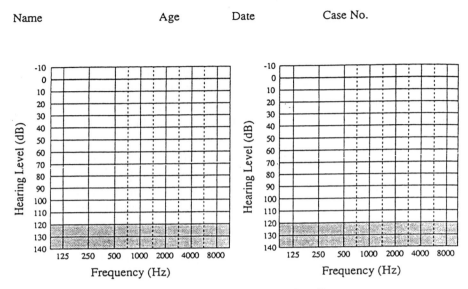

Masking Details   Masking Details

	Right	Left
Air conduction, masked if necessary	O	✕
Air conduction, not masked (shadow point)	●	✗
Bone conduction, not masked	△	
Bone conduction, masked	⊏	⊐
Uncomfortable loudness level	L	⌋

Remarks

Audiometer   Calibration standards   AC   BC   Tested by

Figure 3.7

is a substantial difference between left and right when both ears, using masking, will be tested. The purpose of the bone-conduction test is to measure the sensitivity of the inner ear and the auditory nerve. By comparing your air and bone conduction thresholds, the otologist will be able to determine just where your hearing is impaired. If, for example, your bone conduction is normal but your air conduction is not, the trouble may be assumed to be some form of conductive impairment arising in either the outer or the middle ear. The threshold for bone conduction can never be lower than that for air conduction. With bone conduction a masking sound is usually presented to the opposite ear to ensure that the pure tone will only be perceived in the ear being tested.

Speech Testing

Helen Keller declared that *the sound of the human voice is the most vital stimulus of all* because, as she says, *it brings language, sets thoughts astir and keeps us in the intellectual company of man.* To discover what practical handicap for understanding speech results from the hearing disability, and the extent to which residual hearing can be used for everyday communication, it is necessary to supplement the information obtained from pure-tone tests by speech audiometry.

The procedures for speech audiometry are not very dissimilar to those for pure-tone testing. They basically consist of varying the intensity at which word or sentence lists are presented to each ear in turn, either by pre-recorded tapes or the live voice. The results of these tests are charted on a speech audiogram. One technique that differs from the pure-tone procedures is free-field testing, when the words are delivered at a measured level of loudness by a loudspeaker rather than through headphones. Free-field testing is especially useful in helping to gauge the likely benefit of a hearing aid in normal circumstances.

The most important information obtained from speech audiometry is concerned with: your Speech Reception Threshold or SRT; your Speech Discrimination Score or PB; (phonetic balance) your Most Comfortable Loudness Level or MCL; your Threshold or Discomfort or TD.

Ascertaining your SRT and PB Score

The SRT is the lowest decibel level at which you can correctly score 50 per cent of a list of either monosyllable or spondee words. (A *spondee* is a word of two syllables in which equal stress is laid on each syllable, e.g. *birth-day, head-light*). This level of approximates closely to the average of your thresholds for frequencies of 500, 1000 and 2000 Hz. As with pure tone audiometry, your speech reception threshold represents a comparison of your hearing for speech with the SRT of people with *normal* hearing.

Speech Discrimination tests are even more helpful in measuring socially useful hearing. They are also of great value in distinguishing between conductive and sensorineural losses and in the prescription of suitable hearing aids. The words we use in speech are made up from speech sounds. These speech sounds consist of either consonants or vowels, and in English 16 vowel and 22 consonant sounds can be identified. Vowel sounds are easier to hear because they are lower in frequency and higher in intensity than consonants. Between the loudest vowel sound *aw* and the softest consonant sound *th* there is a difference of almost 30 dB. In testing for intelligibility it would be ideal to use isolated speech sounds, but unfortunately these cannot be produced without considerable distortion. So the tester uses either lists of monosyllabic words or short sentences in which the speech sounds occur with the same relative frequency as they do in ordinary spoken English. Such lists are called phonetically balanced or PB lists. While, in principle, sentence tests are closer to the speech we all try to hear in everyday life, it has been found that in practice there is a close correlation between tests using sentences and single-word tests. Single-word tests are therefore used for speed and convenience and sentence tests are valuable for people with a severe hearing loss who cannot understand speech at all without considerable help from the context.

In Britain the most widely used tests for speech audiometry are those developed by Fry, Boothroyd and the Medical Research Council. The BKB (Bench, Kowal and Bamford) sentence tests are also widely used.

Fry sentence and word articulation tests were developed by D B Fry when Professor of Experimental Phonetics at London University. The sentence tests consist of 10 lists each of 25 sentences. The word articulation tests had 10 lists, each with 35 words of which 30 are of the consonant–vowel–consonant type and 5 either consonant–vowel or vowel–consonant.

Word List 1 of the Fry articulation test comprises the following:

cut	hear	raw	hut	more
sin	keys	tin	ten	thick
bite	lid	sack	less	
will	deaf	men	face	
bone	yard	wish	so	
now	pays	ton	choice	
am	while	good	veal	
wrong	heard	dip	there	

Fry tests are scored on the number of words correctly repeated.

Boothroyd (AB) tests were compiled in 1968 by Arthur Boothroyd of Manchester University and comprise lists of 10 words. The main differences between the Fry and Boothroyd lists, apart from their length, is that all the words in the latter are of the consonant–vowel–consonant type and are scored on the basis of the number of speech sounds (phonemes) rather than the number of words correct.

Word List 1 of the AB tests consists of the following

ship	haze	jot
rug	dice	move
fan	both	
cheek	well	

Medical Research Council (MRC) word lists comprise 25 words scored by whole word recognition. Each list of 25 words is prefaced by a trial run of 5 words. MRC Word List 1 comprises

Trial Words

yore	touch	frost	all	pet

Test Words

splash	smile	toe	is	like
lunge	cane	rag	use	no
cleanse	there	grow	then	rub
hook	folk	are	feast	docks
bad	hive	dish	clove	pants

The BKB Sentence Lists are scored on the basis of key words. These tests, while possibly more listener friendly than single words, are more time consuming to score. Each test comprises 16 sentences. For reasons of space only the first four sentences of Test 1 are given.

> The *clown* had a *funny face.*
> The *car engine's running.*
> *She cut* with her *knife.*
> *Children like strawberries.*

A general guide for the evaluation of word discrimination scores is shown in Figure 3.8.

Score	Evaluation
90–100%	Normal limits
75–90%	Slight difficulty comparable to listening over a telephone
60–75%	Moderate difficulty
50–60%	Poor discrimination, difficulty following conversation
Below 50%	Very poor discrimination, difficulty in following running speech

Figure 3.8. Evaluation of Word Discrimination Scores in PB Tests

The Most Comfortable Loudness (MCL) Test

This indicates for each ear, or both ears together when obtained by free field testing, the number of dB above the reference speech reception threshold (SRT) at which you can most easily understand speech. For people with normal hearing this will be about 40 dB above their SRT. The normal SRT is 10 to 10 dB above the normal pure tone threshold at 500, 1000 and 2000 Hz. (Free field testing is a listening condition in which speech (or sound) is presented through loudspeakers in an environment that is totally free of reverberation from nearby surfaces.)

The Threshold of Discomfort

As the term implies, your threshold of discomfort (TD) is the number of dB above zero SRT at which speech becomes uncomfortably loud or even painful. By subtracting your SRT from your TD the tester can ascertain your *dynamic range*. This indicates the range of useful hearing you have in each ear and for both ears when a free field test is given.

These speech tests obviously provide information that is vital both for diagnosing and helping to overcome a hearing impairment through the fitting of a suitable aid. Someone with an uncomplicated conductive impairment will understand speech if the sound is made loud enough. With a sensorineural impairment, however, increased sound may result in still further educed intelligibility due to *recruitment*. Recruitment is a disproportionate increase in the sensation of *loudness* following a slight increase in the intensity of sound. In an ear in which recruitment is absent the MCL will be about 40 dB above the speech reception threshold. When recruitment is present, the MCL may be only 10 dB above the SRT. Where recruitment is marked, an increase of 15–20 dB above the SRT may cause discomfort. Clearly this factor is of considerable importance when considering what help you will receive from a hearing aid.

The Measurement of Hearing Disability

The World Health Organisation makes useful distinctions between the terms impairment, disability and handicap.

Impairment is an anatomical, pathological or psychological loss or defect describable in diagnostic or symptomatic terms.

Disability is a limitation of performance in once or more activities which are generally accepted as essential basic components of daily living such that partial or complete inability to perform them necessitates a degree of dependence on a compensatory aid and/or another person.

Handicap comprises the disadvantages or restrictions of activity experienced by an individual as a result of the impairment or disability.

These distinctions become clearer when applied to a specific case. Mr X is a bank clerk with a progressive hearing loss. Defective hearing is his *impairment*.

He has difficulty in hearing normal conversation so that he cannot deal with customers. This is his *disability*.

Because of his disability X's promotion opportunities are restricted. He is therefore *handicapped*. If X can largely overcome his hearing loss by using a hearing aid he will have an impairment but not necessarily a disability or handicap. If, however, the hearing aid makes his impairment visible, this might still prejudice his chances of promotion. Although the disability has been largely overcome, he is still handicapped.

The results of audiometric tests provide the basis for an assessment of the degree of hearing impairment, disability or handicap experienced by a person at a given time. For practical purposes, it is often necessary to equate the quantitative measurement of hearing impairment shown by pure tone and speech audiograms with a given degree of disability. Such practical purposes include compensation for industrial injury and decisions regarding an individual's suitability for certain employments where good hearing is essential. They also include the feasibility of rehabilitation through surgery or the fitting of a hearing aid.

Decisions of the above nature must also take other factors into account such as the likely course of the impairment, the presence of tinnitus and vertigo, and whether both ears are affected.

The first essential is to decide what amount of hearing loss will constitute a given degree of disability. One such classification (formulated by the Committee on Conservation of Hearing of the American Academy of Ophthalmology and Otolaryngology base on pure tone audiometry) is shown in Figure 3.9.

Classes of Hearing Handicap

Hearing Threshold Level (ISO)	Class	Degree of handicap	Average Hearing Threshold Level for 500, 1000 and 2,000 Hz in better ear		Ability to Understand Speech
			more than	not more than	
	A	not significant		25 dB (ISO)	no significant difficulty with faint speech
25					
	B	slight handicap	25 dB (ISO)	40 dB	difficulty only with faint speech
40					
	C	mild handicap	40 dB (ISO)	55 dB	frequent difficulty with normal speech
55					
	D	marked handicap	55 dB	70 dB	frequent difficulty with loud speech
70					
	E	severe handicap	70 dB	90 dB	can understand only shouted or amplified speech
90	F	extreme handicap	90 dB		usually cannot understand even amplified speech

Figure 3.9

A second interesting classification which relates hearing loss as shown by a pure tone audiogram to the ability to hear conversational speech at given distances is that shown in Figure 3.10 by S R Mawson, a British otologist.

Clinical Classification of Deafness

Classification	Social Difficulty Difficulty	Clinic Voice Test	Pure Tone Audiogram
Normal Hearing	none	18 ft or more	no loss over 10 dB
Slight Deafness	long-distance speech	not over 12ft	10–30 db loss
Moderate Deafness	short-distance speech	not over 3ft	up to 60 db loss
Severe Deafness	all unamplified voices	raised voice at meatus	over 60 db loss
Total Deafness	voices never	nil	over 90 db loss

Source: S R Mawson, *Diseases of the Ear* (by permission of the author)

Figure 3.10

A crude relationship between hearing loss and difficulty in social situations is as follows

Hearing Loss	Disability
0–25 dB	Little difficulty in normal situations
25–40 dB	Impairment for church or theatre
40–50 dB	Difficulty in direct conversation
55+	Difficulty with the telephone
90+	Total deafness for speech

Finally, the British Society of Audiology provides the following four descriptions of hearing loss based on the average pure tone hearing thresholds at 250, 500, 1000, 2000 and 4000 Hz.

Audiometric Descriptor	dB HL
Mild hearing loss	
Moderate hearing loss	20–40
Severe hearing loss	41–70
Profound hearing loss	71–95
	in excess of 95

Clearly the above estimates of the difficulties caused will be influenced by factors such as the noise in the environment, the acoustics of a building and the extent to which speech discrimination is affected by a particular ear condition.

Interpreting Audiograms

The interpretation of audiograms is the province of the otologist and there are two reasons why it is dangerous for the layman to venture into this field. First,

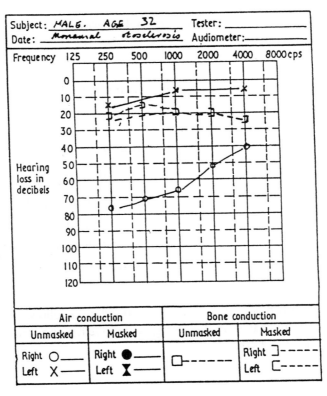

Figure 3.11 Conductive impairments

an audiometric configuration may be the result of more than one cause; it is also necessary to consider the pure-tone audiogram together with a patient's case history and the signs and symptoms observed at the physical examination of his ears, nose and throat. Supplementary information will be obtained when necessary from speech and impedance audiometry. Second, the audiogram of an individual does not always correspond to a *typical* pattern for a particular type of impairment.

Figure 3.11 is the pure-tone audiogram of a man with a conductive impairment due to otosclerosis in the right ear. It will be seen that at the time of the test the left ear was normal for all practical purposes. The bone-conduction curve for the right ear shows a characteristic pattern called the *Carhart notch*. An American otologist, Raymond Carhart, in 1951 reported that prior to surgery, at that time the fenestration operation, the bone conduction of people with otosclerosis could not be measured precisely because of an *inner ear conductive block* caused by the fixed stapes impeding the movement of the inner-ear fluids. On average this impedance results in a lowering of the bone-conduction threshold of 5 dB at 500 Hz, 10 dB at 1000 Hz, 15 dB at 2000 Hz and 20 dB at 4000 Hz. It will be seen that on this audiogram the average losses reported by Carhart have been exceeded.

The difference between the bone and air conduction thresholds is the *bone–air gap* and is a good indication of conductive impairment. If middle-ear surgery is recommended for the restoration of hearing, its principal aim is the reduction or elimination of this gap. Most conductive audiograms show a *flat* curve for the air-conduction losses, with the greater losses occurring in the lower frequencies. While in this audiogram the flatness is not as pronounced as is often the case, the loss in the lower frequencies is clearly shown. By averaging the losses at frequencies of 500, 1000 and 2000 Hz as 70 + 65 + 50 = 62 we can estimate that the speech threshold in this case will be about 62 dB.

Sensorineural Impairments

Figures 3.12 and 3.13 show the pure-tone audiograms of two cases of sensorineural impairment. Figure 3.12 is the audiogram of a man aged 64 with presbyacusis, while Figure 3.13 refers to a woman aged 56 with Méniére's Disease. In the former case it will be seen that the bone and air conduction thresholds are approximately equal, which is indicative of a sensorineural loss. In both instances there is near normal hearing at the lower frequencies with a fairly steep fall in the higher ranges. The practical effect is that while the lower-pitched vowel sounds will still be audible, there will be difficulty in hearing the higher-pitched consonant sounds.

Figure 3.14 is the speech audiogram of another case of otosclerosis.

The speech discrimination curve for a person with normal hearing is shown for comparison on the left. It will be seen that the speech discrimination score or PB curve is very similar to that for normal hearing except that it is necessary to elevate the intensity level by the amount of hearing loss. In this case the intensity level had to be raised to 60 dB before a 100 per cent score was obtained. Persons with this type of pure conductive loss are ideal candidates for hearing aids.

Figure 3.15 is the speech audiogram of a person with a sensorineural loss. (Again the speech discrimination curve for a person with normal hearing is shown on the left.) Not until the intensity level is raised to about 65 dB will 50 per cent of the words comprising the test be correctly heard. At between 75 dB and 90 dB the score improves to approximately 62%. After this point, discrimination deteriorates as amplification increases; thus, if the intensity level is raised to 95 dB, the score declines to about 55 per cent. Parabolic curves are never found in

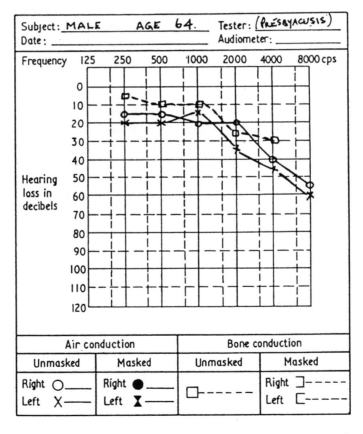

Figure 3.12

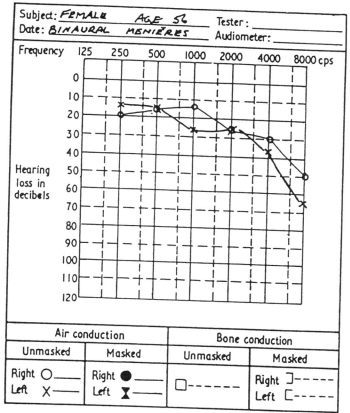

Subject: *FEMALE* AGE *56* Tester: _____
Date: *BINAURAL MENIÈRES* Audiometer: _____

Figure 3.13

pure conductive losses; they do, however, illustrate the effect of recruitment and the importance of this factor for the prescription and dispensing of hearing aids.

Impedance Audiometry

An impedance audiometer is an instrument for the measurement of acoustic immittance. This term requires some explanation. *Immittance* is a general term which, in physics, includes both admittance and impedance. Admittance is the ease with which energy flows through a system. Impedance is the total opposition to energy flow in a system. In acoustic terms admittance and impedance are respectively the ability of the hearing system to absorb or resist sound energy. Sound energy, as we have seen, causes the ear drum to vibrate. Sound is then conducted across the middle ear by the ossicles and transmitted to the cochlea in the inner ear by the rocking of the stapes in the oval window. In a health ear there will be minimum impedance and maximum admittance or *compliance* to the

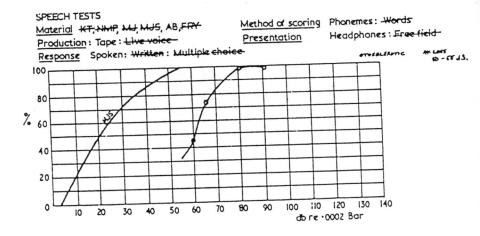

Figure 3.14

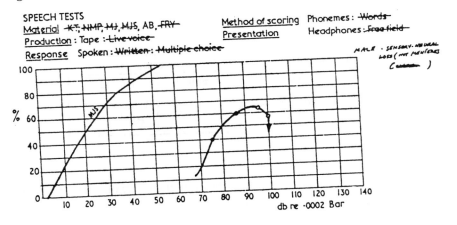

Figure 3.15

flow of sound energy. If, however, the system is functioning imperfectly due to such causes as inadequate ventilation of the middle ear by the Eustachian tube or reduced stapes mobility as in otosclerosis, there will be increased impedance and reduced compliance, resulting in less sound being received by the cochlea because more sound energy will be reflected from the ear drum back into the ear canal.

By means of an impedance or *acoustic immittance* audiometer, the otologist can assemble reliable and objective information regarding the functioning of your middle ear mechanism comprising your ear drum, Eustachian tube and ossicular chain.

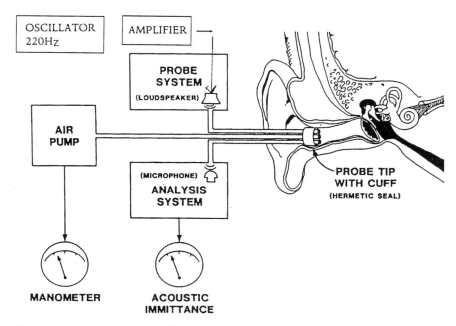

Figure 3.16. Basic Workings of an Impedance Audiometer

The basic workings of an impedance audiometer are shown in Figure 3.16.

The impedance audiometer comprises (1) a headset, (2) a probe connected to (3) an impedance bridge with two dials, a manometer to record air pressure in the ear canal and a balance meter for measuring acoustic immittance. In impedance testing the probe is inserted into the ear canal and hermetically sealed by a plug or cuff. The outer and middle ears then form two counties divided by the ear drum.

The tip of the probe has three openings connected respectively by find rubber tubes to the loudspeaker, air pump and acoustic immittance meter.

A standard tone of 220 Hz (65 dB) is fed by the probe into the ear canal and causes the ear drum to vibrate.

When the air pressure on each side of the drum is equal, movement of the ear drum will be minimal and there will be minimum impedance so that little sound energy will be reflected back into the ear canal. If, however, there is any impedance, some of the sound energy will be reflected back into the ear canal. The greater the impedance, the greater the energy reflected. The amount of sound energy reflected rather than transmitted through the middle ear will be picked up by the microphone and conveyed to the acoustic meter and measured according to the type of instrument, either in volts or cubic centimetres of equivalent volume.

The air pump is used to vary the air pressure in the ear canal. These variances in air pressure are indicated by the manometer. The changes in compliance that occur as the air pressure is varied can be read on the balance meter and plotted on a graph or *tympanogram*.

Modern impedance audiometers are automatic in operation and have easy to read displays that show test results in real time in addition to providing printouts.

Applications of Impedance Audiometry

Impedance audiometry assembles a number of individual tests into a *battery* that enables the otologist to identify a *pattern* recognizable as relating to a distinct clinical condition. Two important tests in this battery are tympanometry and the ascertainment of acoustic reflex thresholds.

Tympanometry

Tympanometry has been defined as *the measurement of effect of varying air pressure on the mobility of the middle ear system.* These changes as shown by a tympanogram indicate the effect on compliance of varying the air pressure in the air-tight external ear from -200 mm water pressure +0 +200 mm water pressure. (The chemical symbol H_2O is used to avoid the repetition of the term *water pressure.*) As indicated by Figure 3.17 all tympanograms have three identifiable features: (1) a pressure peak; (2) an amplitude (extent of vibratory movement from extreme to extreme); and (3) a shape.

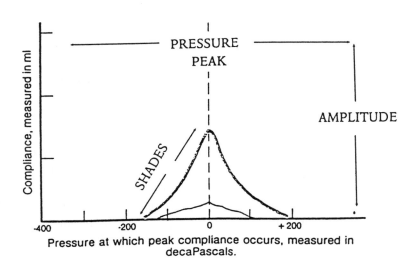

Figure 3.17. A Normal Tympanogram

The *location* of the pressure peak provides the otologist with information regarding middle ear ventilation. As we have seen, there will be maximum compliance when there is equal air pressure on both sides of the ear drum. Peak compliance will be at 0 mm H2O. The peak of the tympanogram therefore provides a good guide to the air pressure in the middle ear.

Amplitude gives information regarding the static impedance of the ear, in other words, the volume of air in the middle ear cavity only.

The *shape* of the tympanogram may be considered as a revelation of altered resonance or internal noise in the middle ear system. Tympanograms take number of shapes classified for convenience into three main categories (A, B and C) with two A and B subcategories. Some of these shapes are shown by Figure 3.18. The B subcategories are not shown in Figure 3.18.

Acoustic Reflex Testing

This is another important application of impedance audiometry. In Chapter 2 reference was made to the stapedius muscle. When presented with an acoustic signal of sufficient intensity and duration this muscle stiffens, thus helping to protect the inner ear mechanism from the effects of loud noise. In normal ears this stiffening or contraction takes place at an intensity of about 85 dB. The contraction increases the impedance of the ear and can be measured by the impedance audiometer.

Even though a sound greater than the normal sound is presented to only one ear, the stapedius muscles contract in both ears. It is, therefore, possible to record both ipsilateral and contralateral reflexes. An ipsilateral reflex occurs when a pure tone is presented by the probe to the ear under test. A contralateral reflex takes place when a pure tone is presented by a headset to the ear not being tested. With normal hearing, two possible reflexes, one ipsilateral and one contralateral can be obtained for each ear.

The absence or presence of reflexes, the intensity at which they occur and their pattern provides the otologist with much useful diagnostic information. In general, where a reflex is present, it indicates that the ossicles are mobile; with most middle ear impairments the ability to monitor reflexes is obliterated. If contraction takes place only in response to a signal greater than 85 dB, it is usually indicative of conductive loss in the ear under test. Reflex testing can also be used to obtain information regarding Acoustic Reflex Decay or the ability of the middle ear to maintain a contraction. Where the ear is normal, the acoustic reflex will be maintained over a 10 second period, at 10 dB above the reflex threshold level at 500 and 1000Hz. If there is a reducation in amplitude of 50 per cent or greater within five seconds, there is an indication of a retrocochlear lesion such as an VIIIth nerve tumour or brain stem disorder.

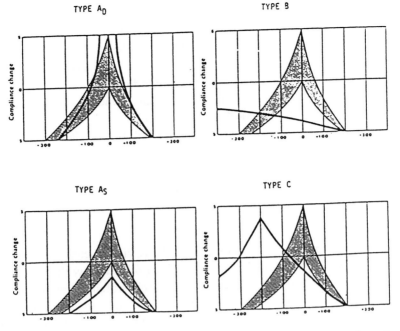

Figure 3.18. Shape and Classification of Tmpanograms. The shaded areas show the range for normally mobile ears. A plot within that area is called Type A.

Type A$_D$ (the D stands for *deep*)	indicates that normal middle ear pressure is present but compliance is unusually high. This pattern tends to occur when the ear drum is flaccid. If compliance is greater than 5 cm^3 it is an indication of ossicular discontinuity.
Type A$_S$ (the S stands for *shallow*)	again indicates normal middle ear pressure but reduced mobility of the ear drum. The shallow, i.e. less than 0.3 cm^3, curve suggests a fixation of the ossicles as occurs with otosclerosis or adhes-sions due to serious otitis media.
Type B	Here the peak is absent and compliance values over the whole pressure range are almost equal. This configuration is often found when the middle ear is filled with fluid.
Type C	In this configuration shifting of the peak to the negative range, typically -100 mm H$_2$O or more, indicates that although compliance values are normal there is negative pressure in the middle ear. This is because through blockage the Eustachian tube is not fulfilling its function of equalizing air pressure in the middle ear.

Taking an Impedance Test

Although the above description is somewhat detailed, impedance testing is simple and can be expeditiously undertaken. Unlike pure tone or speech testing, it requires little response from you. Impedance testing is, in fact, particularly useful in situations where it is difficult to obtain responses as is the case with very young children.

The person administering the test may ask you to open your mouth wide while he draw your auricle slightly upwards and backwards. This procedure enables the probe to be inserted comfortably in your ear. Your ear channel will be made airtight by an appropriately sized plug.

Tympanometry will precede reflex testing. Both the continuous and pulsed tones are recorded on a Békeséy audiogram on which solid lines represent thresholds obtained with a continuous line and dashed lines threshold results with intermittent or pulsed tones. A pulsed tone is an interrupted sound which is *pulsed* rapidly on and off.

The configurations of a Békeséy audiogram provide the otologist with information regarding recruitment and the nature and site of hearing loss. Recruitment, for example, causes the width of the continuous tracing on the audiogram to diminish, indicating greater sensitivity to small changes in intensity. The superimposition of continuous and pulsed tracings on each other occurs with normal hearing or in conductive losses. Conversely, a pattern in which at frequencies of about 1000 Hz the continuous tone falls to approximately 20 dB below the intermittent tone and then runs parallel to it into the higher frequencies, is indicative of cochlear impairment such as Méniére's disease or presbyacusis.

Békeséy audiometry is being largely replaced by Evoked Response Audiometry which provides greater confidence in diagnosis, particularly in respect of retrocochlear disorders. (A retrocochlear disorder is one sited *beyond the cochlea*, i.e. affecting the auditory nerve and brain stem.) An *auditory evoked response* is activity – a response, within the auditory system (the ear, the auditory nerve or auditory region of the brain) that is *evoked* or produced by sounds, i.e. auditory or acoustic stimuli. Brain activity, *brainwaves*, evoked by a stimulus of very short duration termed a *click* is picked up by electrodes placed on the forehead or ear lobe. The activity evoked by the *click* arises from structures within the ear, nerve and brain at some distance from the skin electrodes. This sensory and neural activity is conveyed from its origin through body tissues and fluids to the surface electrodes. These wires convey the electrical activity to a specially programmed computer which adds and averages the signals picked up by the electrodes.

The two main forms of evoked response audiometry are electrocochleography and brain stem electric response audiometry.

In *electrocochleography* the patient is given a local or, in the case of children, general anaesthetic. This allows a needle electrode to be passed through the ear drum and held in place against the promontory near the round window. The responses provide reliable information regarding the functioning of the cochlea and the acoustic nerve.

Brain stem electric response audiometry provides similar information to electrocochleography. It only requires the electrodes to be placed on the skull and is therefore non-invasive. Because of this relative ease of application it is increasingly preferred to electrocochleography although it is possible to use both techniques. In both approaches the otologist is assisted in his diagnosis by a study of the time intervals in milliseconds between the stimulus *click* and response and the amplitude and shape of the wave forms of responses as shown on an electro-encephalogram (ECG).

One advantage of evoked response audiometry is that the results obtained are objective and independent of the patient's responses. It is therefore the most reliable way of predicting hearing thresholds in infants. Brain stem audiometry has also applications in the early detection of multiple sclerosis and acoustic tumours. Evoked response audiometry is clearly of great importance in determining the suitability of potential candidates for cochlear implants. Not all implant centres use this procedure.

4

You and Your Otologist

The most constructive advice that can be given to someone with any form of ear trouble is to seek an appointment with an otologist. If you have ear trouble you should also do so if a considerable number of years has elapsed since last you saw an ear specialist. It is just possible that you might be helped by developments that have taken place in the interim. Accurate information on the type of loss and its cause is essential before a person with a hearing loss can be helped. Only otologists, often working as a team, can assemble the required data.

How does an ear specialist arrive at a diagnosis of what is wrong and determine what steps might be taken to cure or at least ameliorate an ear condition?

Visiting the Otologist

The protocol is that you should ask your general practitioner to give you a letter of introduction to an ear specialist. If you feel you need advice on your ear trouble do not be dissuaded. Not all general practitioners are interested in ears or keep abreast of progress in this field and people with treatable hearing conditions have sometimes been wrongly advised that nothing can be done for them. Syringing and eardrops will only relieve a loss of hearing due to wax in the outer ear.

Your doctor should know who is the best available ear specialist for you to see. The more knowledgeable a doctor is about ears the more information he or she will have about the reputations of otologists. There is nothing to stop you asking to be referred to a consultant of your own choice. Your doctor may arrange for you to see an ear specialist without cost at the outpatients department of a hospital. Under the National Health Service, however, you have no automatic right to see a particular consultant at an outpatients clinic. You may, alternatively, prefer to see the consultant privately, in which case a fee will be payable.

While ultimately you would expect the diagnosis and treatment to be the same, I believe that it is more informative to see the otologist privately, at least for the first visit. This does not imply any criticism of the National Health Service; it is simply based on the personal experience that in a busy hospital clinic otologists have less time to explain the nature of your ear condition and to answer the questions you will want to ask than they have in the quietness of their consulting rooms where there are far fewer distractions.

The consultant will be listed in the Medical Directory or the Medical Register (available in most public reference libraries). He or she will almost certainly hold the Fellowship of one of the three Royal Colleges of Surgeons (London, Edinburgh or Dublin). The convention is that a male surgeon is addressed as Mr, a physician as Dr.

The Otologist's Diagnosis

Like detectives, otologists seek their clues from three sources: the victim, the site of the crime and independent witnesses. The first clues come from the victim – yourself. The otologist will want information that only you can provide. To save time at the consultation you should reflect on the following questions before your visit.

(1) Which of the following symptoms are present:

    (a) hearing loss

    (b) head noises

    (c) dizziness

    (d) discharge from the ear

    (e) earache.

(2) For how long have I been troubled by the symptoms?

(3) What event(s) do I associate with the onset of my ear condition (e.g. an accident, colds, noise, pregnancy, worry)?

(4) Have any members of my family had impaired hearing?

(5) Do I hear better in a noisy situation?

(6) Do I find loud noises or speech uncomfortable?

The helpfulness of your answers will be enhanced if you have given them some further consideration. For example, grandfather's deafness which only became marked in his eighties was probably due to presbyacusis and is not significant. Aunt Marie who 'went deaf' at 30 is worth reporting. It is also helpful to the consultant if you can explain in simple terms not merely that you have tinnitus but whether it is intermittent or continuous, affects one or both ears, and what sounds the head noises resemble.

The consultant will also note certain 'give away' clues such as those mentioned in Chapter 2 namely whether you speak loudly or softly, strain to catch what is said or try to lip read conversation.

The second set of clues will be obtained from an examination of your ears, nose and throat. The otologist will be particularly interested in your ear drums and Eustachian tubes. He will note whether the ear drums are normal or if they are perforated; in otitis media the drums may bulge outward or be drawn inwards. Changes in the colour and texture of the drums may also provide clues to what is wrong. Similarly, the consultant will want to know whether your Eustachian tubes are functioning efficiently. You may be asked to pinch your nostrils and puff out your cheeks so that the effect on your hearing and ear-drums can be checked. The otologist will also examine your nose and throat for abnormalities that may cause ear trouble or aggravate an existing condition.

The third set of clues will be obtained from audiometric or tuning-fork tests. Before audiometers, otologists had to rely on tuning forks to determine the upper and lower tone limits within the speech range, and distinguish between conductive and sensorineural impairments.

The three most important tuning-fork tests are known as Weber, Rinne and Schwabach after their originators. The Weber test is used to determine whether hearing impairment affecting only one ear is conductive or perceptive, by comparing the bone conduction of both ears. A vibrating tuning fork is placed in the middle of the forehead. The person under test is asked to state whether he hears the sound in his good or his impaired ear. If the sound is heard in the impaired ear the bone conduction must be better in this ear than the other and the trouble will be conductive. If the sound is heard better in the good ear the hearing loss in the opposite ear will be sensorineural.

The Rinne test depends on the fact that with normal hearing a tuning fork held close to the ear will be heard (by air conduction) for about twice as long as one placed on the mastoid (heard by bone conduction). A vibrating fork is therefore held just outside the ear passage. When the person under test no longer hears the vibrations the fork is transferred to the mastoid. Both ears are tested in this way. If the vibrations are heard longer by bone than by air conduction, that is evidence of a conductive impairment.

The Schwabach test compares the bone conduction of a person with a hearing difficulty to that of someone assumed to have normal hearing. The vibrating tuning fork is placed on the patient's mastoid. When the vibrations are no longer heard the fork is immediately transferred to the otologist's mastoid. If the otologist continues to hear the vibrations it suggests that the patient has a sensorineural loss.

Although the Weber, Rinne and Schwabach tests are still used, otologists now prefer to rely on the information obtained from the pure tone, speech, impedance and other audiometric tests described in Chapter 3. The advantage of the above and other audiological procedures are many. The results of such tests are quantitative and objective rather than qualitative and subjective; audiograms and tympanograms show the pattern of hearing impairment by enabling typical configurations to be identified; the graphs can be kept by the otologist and used to measure either the extent of deterioration or changes over a given period and the degree of improvement resulting from treatment; the records can easily be transferred to a new consultant; audiograms can be used to prescribe the type of hearing and treatment most likely to benefit a particular person.

If vertigo is one of your symptoms the otologist will also test your balance. Balance tests range from simple procedures requiring you to close your eyes and stand still either with your feet together or marking time or walking heel to toe along a straight line, to caloric tests in which your outer ear is irrigated with water 7 per cent above and later 7 per cent below body temperature. This causes nystagmus (a condition in which there is involuntary movement to the eyes) which can be observed either directly by the otologist or electrically recorded by a method called electronystagmography. Positional vertigo may be tested by asking you to lie on a bed with your head placed backwards and to one side while the otologist watches your reactions.

It must be stressed, however, that neither tuning fork or audiometric testing do anything more than provide evidence of the probable type and site of hearing impairment. The otologist can only form a reliable diagnosis, prognosis and decide what can be done, when the above tests have been considered in association with the clues provided by yourself and an examination of your ears, nose, throat and, where appropriate, balance.

What can the Otologist do?

When treating your ear condition the otologist will seek to achieve one or more of the following objectives: the elimination of infection; the restoration or improvement of hearing; the relief of associated problems such as vertigo or tinnitus.

The Elimination of Infection

As explained in Chapter 2, most acute infections of the middle ear are due to bacteria spreading up the Eustachian tube as a result of colds, tonsillitis and similar conditions. Before about 1938, acute otitis media was attended by the very real danger that an infection of the middle ear might invade the mastoid process and, unless relieved by prompt surgery, result in such potentially fatal complications as meningitis or a brain abscess.

Many older people will recall at school contemporaries who 'had a mastoid' and ugly-looking scars behind the ears to prove it.

To prevent the accumulation of pus and the perforation of the ear drum the usual procedure was **myringotomy**, the surgeon making an incision in the ear drum for the double purpose of relieving pain and allowing the fluid to escape. Myringotomy is still occasionally performed when other procedures fail to give relief, especially when the Eustachian tube is blocked with the result that the middle ear is inadequately ventilated. In the latter case the otologist may insert a small dumbbell-like tube or 'grommet' through myringotomy to prevent the absorption by the middle ear's mucous membrane of the remaining air and its replacement by fluid. The grommet maintains atmospheric pressure in the middle ear, and when the drum is retracted the insertion of the tube usually leads to an improvement in hearing.

The dramatic fall in the incidence of mastoid infection and its complications since 1938 has been due to the effects of sulpha drugs and antibiotics. Their advent revolutionized otology, as it did most other branches of medicine. Far fewer myringotomies were needed, since antibiotics given early in otitis media control the infection so that the condition resolves without rupture of the ear drum. Even if a perforation has taken place the ear drum heals with minimal scarring so that the hearing is not permanently impaired. The emergency mastoid operation ceased to be commonplace. Many ear conditions that had formerly required the attention of the specialist otologist could be treated as a matter of routine by the general practitioner. The knowledge that infection could be controlled gave otologists the confidence to develop modern surgical procedures for the ear.

There are, however, complications in the use of antibiotics. One such complication, the so called 'glue ear', has already been mentioned in the discussion of otitis media in Chapter 2. Another danger is that the use of the antibiotic may be discontinued before it has completely eliminated the infection. When an antibiotic has been prematurely abandoned the re-emergence of resistant strains of bacteria is encouraged. It appears that the fire has been put out, but the underlying infection is smouldering, ready to flare up later in the form of 'masked mastoiditis' with its attendant dangers. The need for surgery for the removal or prevention of ear infections has not been entirely eliminated by the use of antibiotics. A familiar example is the removal of chronically affected adenoids that may be responsible for the infection or obstruction of the Eustachian tube.

The Restoration or Improvement of Hearing

'There are two kinds of deafness. One is due to wax and is curable, the other is not due to wax and is not curable.'

So declared Sir William Wilde FRCS, the father of Oscar Wilde. William Wilde, one of the first surgeons to take a special interest in otology, lived between

1815 and 1876. Until after World War II his statement was still substantially true except that, as we have seen, the incidence of hearing impairment had been significantly reduced by the use of antibiotics. Especially in the fields of profound congenital deafness and conductive impairments the situation has now changed dramatically due to such factors as the ante-natal screening of mothers, the screening of babies and school children, the development of the science of audiology, the possibilities opened up by operating microscopes, modern anaesthetics, the microchip and the ongoing work of researchers throughout the world. In the UK the Institute of Hearing Research was set up at Nottingham University in 1977 by the Medical Research Council. The objectives of the Institute include, *inter alia*:

> 'To conduct basic research on hearing and deafness that may eventually lead to applications that may improve hearing related aspects of human health.
> To conduct applied research likely to lead in currently envisageable ways to the improvement of health care for people with hearing disorders in the foreseeable future.'

The Hearing Research Trust founded in 1985 is also funding and helping to fund at universities and similar institutions a number of projects aimed at improving the treatment and prevention of deafness and related problems such as tinnitus.

The practical result of the above developments is that today otologists have at their disposal a greatly enhanced armoury of approaches to the relief of hearing impairment due to conductive or sensorineural hearing impairments and of associated conditions such as vertigo and tinnitus.

Conductive Hearing Loss

Examples of what can be done with hearing loss due to conductive impairment can be found in the treatment of injury to the ear drum and the effects of chronic otitis media and the relief of hearing loss arising from otosclerosis.

Injury to the Ear Drum and the Effects of Chronic Otitis Media
Tympanoplasty

Tympanoplasty is the term for a group of procedures aimed at eradicating disease and restoring the sound-conducting mechanism of the middle ear. The procedures involved in tympanoplasty may be subdivided into myringoplasty and ossiculoplasty.

Myringoplasty seeks to repair the ear drum where a perforation is too large to repair by other means. In effect the hole is 'patched' by tissue usually taken from the temporal muscle. Such repairs can, of course, be made only when the ear is free from discharge.

Ossiculoplasty is the reconstruction of the ossicular chain, the three small bones of the middle ear popularly termed the hammer, anvil and stirrup. These may become immobile or broken by disease or injury. Destructive disease in the middle ear, for instance, usually affects the anvil or incus which, being in the centre of the chain, has the worst blood supply. The surgeon may place the patient's own incus in a new position; he may use an artificial replacement for a part of the chain; he may even use replacement ossicles removed from other people in the course of middle-ear operations. Some people actually bequeath their ossicles to be removed after their deaths and used in replacement surgery.

Although attempts to close perforations by surgical means were made in the last century it was not until new approaches to the problem were devised in 1953 by a German surgeon, Horst Wullstein, that interest in tympanoplasty was revived. Since 1953 much as been done to improve the results obtained. Not until the surgeon has inspected the middle ear through the operating microscope, however, can the repairs necessary to restore hearing be precisely determined. Tympanoplasty techniques therefore require great skill, patience and ingenuity from the otologist.

Otosclerosis

Historically, surgical attempts to restore hearing lost through otosclerosis have taken three separate paths: **fenestration, stapes mobilization** and **stapedectomy.**

Fenestration. (Fenestra is the Latin word for 'window'.) This approach attempts to bypass the fixed stapes through the creation of a new window or fenestra in the labyrinth. This window enables sound vibrations to be transmitted via the inner ear fluids to the round window. The first attempt to create a new window was made in 1897, but the improvement in hearing resulting from early efforts was temporary, in most cases lasting for only a few days. It was not until about 1938 that a simplified one-stage operation, developed by Julius Lempert of New York, really put fenestration on the otological map. Some excellent results were obtained by this procedure but there were a number of disadvantages. Fenestration remained a major operation requiring two to three weeks in hospital followed by a lengthy period of outpatient treatment. Often complications such as dizziness and discharge were encountered. Most seriously, hearing tended to deteriorate to the pre-operative level, due to the closure of the fenestra by a new overgrowth of spongy bone. This latter factor was distressing to the patient and frustrating for the otologist.

Mobilization of the stapes was also attempted by early otologists but their poor results and the high danger of serious infection in the pre-antibiotic era led to its abandonment until it was 'accidentally' rediscovered in 1952 by Samuel Rosen of New York. While preparing to perform a fenestration using a local anaesthetic Rosen moved the patient's stapes just as a metal pan fell on the floor in an adjoining room. The patient remarked that he had heard something fall, whereupon Rosen whispered very softly, 'Do you like scrambled eggs?' 'Yes' was the reply 'and I heard every word'.

In a sense, stapes mobilization was the direct opposite of fenestration. It was a much simpler operation requiring only a short stay in hospital and without post-operative complications. Sometimes near-normal hearing could be restored, a considerable advance on the best that could be expected from fenestration. Moreover, even if unsuccessful, stapes mobilization did not preclude a fenestration operation later. The procedure, however, also had its disadvantages. The stapes might become refixed by the pathological process of otosclerosis and there are also dangers in the operation itself. Though initially stapes mobilization tended to be regarded as a 'nothing-to-it' operation in which the stapes was given a little wiggle and hearing was miraculously restored, it soon emerged that great care was needed from the surgeon. If the stapes was moved a little too hard a loss of 60 dB or more could occur, or it might even be pushed further into the inner ear resulting in no hearing at all.

Stapedectomy, involving the complete or partial removal of the stapes has been the most successful operation of all and is now the operation of choice. Like fenestration and stapes mobilization, it had been attempted by earlier otologists and abandoned because of its technical difficulties. It was not until 1956 that John Shea, Jnr, of Tennessee performed the first stapedectomy involving the use of a prosthesis (a prosthesis is an artificial part). In Shea's original operation the stapes was completely removed, the oval window thus being left open and closed by a graft consisting of a small segment of vein removed from the patient's arm. A polythene sheet was then used to bridge the gap between the incus and the vein graft. In 1963 Shea started to use a piston made of Teflon, a plastic material, rather than a polythene sheet. Meanwhile, another American surgeon Schuknecht modified Shea's procedure by sealing the oval window with fat from the patient's ear lobe and using fine stainless steel wire as the piston which was crimped over the incus for extra security. Later developments avoid the complete removal of the stapes by leaving the footplate in position. A small hole is drilled in the footplate just large enough to permit the insertion of a stainless steel or plastic piston which is crimped to the incus.

Stapedectomy is now the standard surgical procedure for the improvement of hearing loss due to otosclerosis. It does not cure the otosclerosis but in the overwhelming majority of cases it does provide long lasting serviceable hearing to people who half a century ago could have had little done for them.

As the operation will be of great interest and importance to many readers of this book, an attempt is made below to answer some of the queries that a person with otosclerosis might wish to raise. The answers given are, of course, no more than generalizations and each person should discuss his or her case with an otologist.

What are the main factors that the otologist considers in determining whether a person is suitable for stapedectomy surgery?

(1) Correct diagnosis.

(2) The state of the nerve of hearing as shown by the difference between the bone and air conduction thresholds. The aim of the operation is in fact to close the gap between hearing by bone and air conduction as shown by an audiogram. Ideally the loss by air conduction should be between 30 and 60 dB.

(3) A speech discrimination score of at least 60 per cent.

(4) Absence of infection.

(5) Good Eustachian tube function in the ear to be treated, as indicated by tympanometry.

(6) The total risk to hearing. If the patient has serviceable hearing in only one ear it is generally unadvisable to take the risk, however slight, of damaging the 'good' ear.

(7) Age.

Is stapedectomy precluded if I am over 60 years of age?

Theoretically, no. Most surgeons are reluctant to operate on persons over 70 years due to the danger of speech discrimination becoming worse because of presbyacusis.

Assuming the otologist considers me suitable for stapedectomy, what in percentage terms are the chances of a substantial improvement in my hearing?

Better than 90 per cent.

Is there any danger that my hearing may be worse after a stapedectomy operation?

Yes. The greatest risk is of a 'dead ear' either at the time of the operation or later. In good hands the risk at operation is small (about 2%). There are, however, cases of hearing loss occurring months or even years after the operation, sometimes for no apparent reason.

What is the alternative to stapedectomy?

The use of a hearing aid. Apart from the reasons mentioned earlier, there may be little point in encouraging an elderly person who has become well adjusted to the use of a hearing aid to undergo stapedectomy. With younger people the abandonment of a hearing aid may be desirable for vocational and social reasons.

If I have a stapedectomy, for how long am I likely to be in hospital and away from work?

Two or three days in hospital and a further one or two weeks away from work.

Is the operation performed under a general or local anaesthetic?

Either, depending on the preferences of the surgeon. Most surgeons seem to prefer general anaesthesia. The present writer, however, had two stapedectomies performed under local anaesthesia and was comfortable throughout – more comfortable, in fact, than during some visits to the dentist.

If the operation is successful will my hearing be restored immediately?

Sometimes there is an immediate hearing improvement that may temporarily disappear. Hearing usually returns in two to four weeks.

Is the hearing improvement likely to be permanent?

Yes, in the overwhelming majority of cases. As stated above, however, there have been cases of hearing loss occurring months or years after an initially successful result. Among the causes of post-operative conductive loss are the slipping of the prosthesis and a leak of inner ear fluid (perilymph) from the oval window.

If the hearing loss does regress after an initially successful stapedectomy, is it possible for the surgeon to rectify matters?

It depends on the reason for the regression. With some cases a so called 'revision' operation is possible. Where the loss is due to the slipping of the prosthesis, for example, the bone–air gap can be restored to within 10 dB in about half of all cases.

If one ear is successfully treated is it possible to perform a stapedectomy on the other ear at a later date?

Yes, but the advisability of doing so is debatable due to the slight danger of late sensorineural loss which in very rare cases might affect both ears. For this reason most surgeons in the UK, unlike the majority of their American and European colleagues, advocate operating on one ear only, thus providing the patient with the safeguard of being able to use a hearing aid in the unoperated ear. A middle of the road view is that at least five years should be allowed to elapse before an operation on the second ear is contemplated.

What is the medical treatment for otosclerosis?

In contrast to the dramatic surgical advances, described above, the only significant development in the medical treatment of otosclerosis has been the widespread acceptance by otologists of sodium fluoride therapy. Fluoride is known to be effective in preventing tooth decay in children. Most natural supplies of drinking water furnish adequate fluoride and those that do not can be fluoridated. Fluoride toothpaste can also remedy deficiencies. Not surprisingly, research has show that osteoporosis (bone softness) is higher in areas where drinking water has a low fluoride content. The incidence of otosclerosis was four times higher in one Australian region with a low fluoride level.

In 1964 Shambaugh and Scott advocated moderate daily doses of sodium fluoride as a means of promoting recalcification and inhibiting the growth of soft spongy bone. Present evidence is that sodium fluoride does little or nothing to improve the hearing loss associated with cochlear otosclerosis. There is, however, evidence that when given in prescribed daily doses for an initial period of two years and thereafter at a reduced strength for life, sodium fluoride stabilizes the sensorineural element of cochlear otosclerosis. In any event, as Beales, an English otologist, has observed, 'at the present time fluoride therapy is the only known method of promoting recalcification and inactivation of an actively expanding focus of otosclerosis'.

Sensorineural Hearing Loss

The restoration or improvement of sensorineural hearing loss is the great challenge now facing otologists. Success in meeting this challenge will only be achieved by the practical application of research findings that broaden our understanding of the hearing processes of the cochlea and the neural pathways to the brain. As stated, the search for such understanding is unremitting. Discoveries in one research centre are taken up and further developed in another. Thus research is international in its scope. To give just one example: at the time of writing a research team at the University of Keele's Department of Communication and Neuroscience has demonstrated that hearing loss due to certain antibiotics and previously regarded as permanent can recover naturally. Earlier, American researchers studying the recovery of hearing in birds following antibiotic-induced hearing loss had found evidence of the regeneration of the sensory hair cells in the cochlea which convert sound vibrations into the electrical impulses which are sent along the acoustic nerve to the brain. The Keele team, using guinea pigs, has discovered that similar regeneration or regrowth of the hair cells occurs in mammals. The next steps are to investigate the precise mechanism underlying such recovery. If this mechanism can be discovered it may then be possible to stimulate the process artificially and so offer effective treatment for hearing loss, at present irreversible, arising from old age, noise and the action of some drugs and antibiotics.

Such treatment lies in the future. Currently the most exciting possibilities for the rehabilitation of persons with severe or profound sensorineural hearing loss are related to cochlear implants. Cochlear implants are so important that they are dealt with in some detail in Chapter 7.

Vertigo

Vertigo and tinnitus, discussed in Chapter 2, may be troublesome and even distressing accompaniments to hearing impairment. Vertigo can occur independently of conditions arising primarily in the ear. It may, for example, be due to such causes as high blood pressure, drugs and virus infections spreading from the nose or throat along the Eustachian tube into the middle and inner ears and giving rise to labyrinthitis. A thorough medical examination is usually required to establish the reason for 'dizziness' or 'lightheadedness'. This examination, will, if necessary be supplemented by an otologic investigation.

While vertigo is not necessarily due to Méniére's disease (MD), the treatment of this condition illustrates some of the approaches that have been made to the relief of dizziness arising from what is technically known as endolymphatic hypertension. These approaches may be classified by the order in which they are usually tried by the otologist either singly or in combination under the headings of diet, drugs and surgical intervention.

Diet

The dietary treatment is to restrict the intake of salt and fluid in an attempt to reduce the excessive water pressure in the endolymphatic sac in the inner ear which is associated with Méniére's disease. Salt is important in this context since its consumption increases the amount of fluid in the body. In general the diet will specify that salt should be eliminated from cooking and discontinued as a condiment. Bacon, kippers, salt butter and other foods with a high salt content should also be avoided. Incidentally, most oven ready frozen foods have a large salt content. Other forms of sodium (sodium chloride is common salt) include bicarbonate of soda which is an important cake ingredient. While the daily intake of fluid should be regulated it should never be less than two pints. While many otologists commence treatment with a salt controlled diet, others are not convinced of the effectiveness of this regimen.

Drugs

Alongside or independent of diet the otologist is likely to prescribe drugs. The drugs prescribed for Méniére's disease can be categorized as antihistamines, vasodilators and diuretics.

Antihistamines are used to combat allergies and are prescribed to sedate or control the vestibular symptoms of MD. Drugs known by such proprietary names as *Avomine, Benadryl* and *Stugeron* are antihistamines.

Vasodilators expand the arteries. These are used for MD on the theory that the supply of endolymph fluid may be affected by blockage of the branch vessels of the internal auditory artery due to over-activity of the central nervous system. The function of vasodilators such as *Serc* is to dilate the auditory artery and its branches with the object of restoring the blood supply and thus normalizing the output of endolymph.

Diuretics increase urine production and thereby reduce the fluid content of the body. Hydrochlorothiazide and Chlorthalidone, marketed respectively under such trade names as *Esidrix* and *Hygroton* are diuretics. All the above drugs have side effects and require careful prescription. The effectiveness of a particular drug varies from one person to another. The drug that suits you best is likely to be found by a process of experimentation. New drugs effective with MD appear quite frequently.

Surgery

The otologist will usually consider surgical intervention only when diet and drugs have failed to give relief. A number of operations have been devised, varying in complexity from the simple insertion of a grommet in the ear drum to selective destruction of the vestibule by ultrasonic radiation. These operations aim to relieve vertigo in one of three ways: the reduction of endolymph pressure; division of the vestibular nerve; the destruction of the vestibular labyrinth.

The benefits of surgery on the endolymphatic sac (Saccus Decompression) are likely to be greatest in the early stages of MD while hearing is fluctuating. An estimated 80–90 per cent of carefully selected cases will experience vertigo relief. In about 50 per cent of these cases hearing will also improve. Tinnitus will, however, be reduced in only about 25 per cent of those treated.

The aim of division of the vestibular nerve is to prevent abnormal sensory vestibular stimuli from reaching the vestibular neurones. The operation is only performed at a few otoneurosurgical centres. While the surgical or medical destruction of the labyrinth almost certainly guarantees relief from vertigo it also results in a total hearing loss in the treated ear.

Tinnitus

Some self-help approaches to the reliefs of tinnitus are outlined in Chapter 2. For an estimated 85 per cent of tinnitus cases, courage and a constructive attitude combined with a sensible life style, relaxation and the support obtained from membership of a tinnitus group will be the cheapest and most effective treatment. For some people, however, tinnitus is so incapacitating and depressive that they require more than the negative advice to 'learn to live with your head noises'. Apart from counselling and psychological regard to the depressive consequences of tinnitus, the otologist can help in three ways: drugs, surgery and masking.

Drugs

Lignocaine (*Xylocaine* and *Xylotox*), a local anaesthetic usually employed in dentistry, injected intravenously or instilled through a grommet into the ear is the drug that has been most successful in the treatment of tinnitus. Reports of treatment indicate that the individual relief obtained varies usually from less than an hour to several days.

The inconvenience of regular injections can be avoided by drugs taken orally. These fall into three classes: lignocaine analogues (an analogue is something that has a 'like function'), anticonvulsants used in the treatment of epilepsy, and sedatives. Lignocaine analogues include tocainide (*Tonocard*) and Mexiletine (*Mexitil*). A considerable number of anticonvulsants have been tried including carbamazepine (*Tegretol*), primidone (*Mysoline*), sodium valproate (*Epilim*) and phenytoin sodium (*Epanutin*). Anticonvulsants have been reported as being ineffective to people who have not first derived benefit from lignocaine. Sedatives prescribed include barbiturates (brand names *Amytal* and *Sodium Amytal*) and benzodiazepines (brand names *Mogadon, Nitradose, Valium*, etc).

In summary, the current position regarding the drug treatment of tinnitus appears to be:

- The use of drugs is appropriate for only a small proportion of people with very severe tinnitus.
- All drugs have side effects; for some people 'the cure may be worse than the disease'.
- The effects of drugs vary from one person to another and according to the type and origin of the tinnitus.
- In general it is advisable that tranquillisers, for example, Valium, Atensine, should be avoided. Some users state that these drugs make tinnitus worse.

Surgery

Tinnitus may, in some cases be relieved as a by-product of surgery for the relief of other ear conditions such as otosclerosis and Méniére's disease. A number of other surgical procedures have been devised for tinnitus, including ligature of the internal jugular vein and cutting the eighth nerve. From the literature it appears that the outcome of surgery in relation to tinnitus is unpredictable. In some cases there will be an improvement while in others tinnitus will be unchanged or worse. This applies whether surgery is undertaken primarily for other ear conditions, for example hearing or vertigo, or directly for the relief of tinnitus.

Surgery is therefore rarely advised for tinnitus alone.

The use of electrical stimulation of the cochlear similar to the procedure for cochlear implants holds out some hope of relief. Where the nerve of hearing has been cut such help is precluded.

Masking

Masking – the obliteration of one sound by another – is a common experience. We cannot hear conversation in heavy traffic or when the sound of the television is above a certain level. It therefore is logical to attempt to 'blot out' or 'mask' tinnitus by a more acceptable sound. Tinnitus can, of course, be masked by a hearing aid or environmental sounds. It is significant that many people find tinnitus more troublesome in quiet surroundings, for example during the night when in bed.

Tinnitus maskers originally developed in the early 1970s by Jack Vernon at the University of Oregon are small sound generators. As shown in Figure 4.1 a typical tinnitus masker resembles a behind the ear hearing aid. There are also combined hearing aids and tinnitus maskers referred to as 'tinnitus instruments'. These tend to be larger and have more controls than tinnitus maskers.

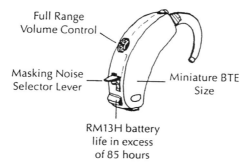

Full Range
Volume Control

Masking Noise
Selector Lever

Miniature BTE
Size

RM13H battery
life in excess
of 85 hours

Figure 4.1. B E Tinitus masker. (Courtesy P.C. Werth)

Tinnitus maskers can be fitted by a hearing aid audiologist once the otologist has eliminated treatment by drugs or surgery. In some cases the otologist may try a combination of drugs and masking.

The procedure for the fitting of a tinnitus masker is very similar to that of a hearing aid. The tester (audiologist, technician or dispenser) will use a pure tone audiometer to obtain information which will enable the quality, pitch and loudness of your tinnitus to be matched.

Quality matching involves presenting pure tones, narrow and broadband noise to discover which most closely resembles your tinnitus. If you have tinnitus in only one ear the noise will be presented to the other ear. Unless the hearing in that ear is too poor for comparison you will be asked to indicate which noise most closely resembles your tinnitus.

For pitch matching the tester will present a tone at one extreme of the audiometer's frequency range and ask you to indicate whether your tinnitus is 'higher' or 'lower'. If, for example, a test tone of 8000 Hz is presented and you indicate that your tinnitus is lower, the tester will start at the other extreme, 125 Hz. You then state that your tinnitus is higher. The tester will then present a tone of 6000 Hz. This process will go on until the extremes are eliminated and the frequency or frequency range corresponding to your tinnitus has been found.

Loudness matching is performed by taking the frequency matched, as described above, with your tinnitus. The test tone will, at first, be presented at the threshold indicated by the audiogram and raised in 5 dB steps until you judge it to be equal in loudness to your tinnitus.

These procedures indicate your minimum masking level (MML). Vernon has pointed out that in general 'the acceptability of tinnitus masking is inversely proportional to its loudness'. The lower the sensation level at which the masking is effective, the more readily does the patient accept it and the greater the relief provided. The aim therefore it to identify the masking sound that effectively masks the tinnitus at the lowest loudness level.

Tinnitus masking is a large subject. Some important findings can be summarized as follows:

- With careful matching, masking can help between 60 and 80 per cent of people with significant tinnitus

- Some cases of tinnitus cannot be helped by masking. These are identified by Vernon as

  (1) those whose hearing is so impaired that they cannot hear the masking sound

(2) those for whom the available masking sound must be presented at un-acceptable loud levels in order to achieve adequate coverage of the tin-nitus; and

(3) those in whom no amount of sound appears to cover the tinnitus.

o Residual inhibition, that is, the temporary suppression of tinnitus after you have taken the masker off, occurs in the majority of cases but varies considerably in duration and may be partial or complete. You should seek advice from the audiologist on the time for which you should use the masker. The higher the level of noise used for masking and the narrower the band of noise presented the shorter the use. Where continuous masking is possible, however, the evidence is that the longer the duration of use the greater the residual inhibition.

o Tinnitus maskers are normally fitted to the affected ear in unilateral tinnitus or the worst affected ear in bilateral tinnitus, unless the hearing loss in that ear is too great for the masking sound to be heard. Binaural tinnitus, however, usually requires a binaural fitting.

o In general an open ear mould should be used to avoid occluding the ear canal. An occluding mould may, however, be needed where the tinnitus is severe or accompanied by a profound hearing loss. In such cases a vented mould should be used.

Apart from cost, features to look for in a tinnitus masker are a volume control adequate to mask the tinnitus and a tone control analogous to the bass/treble control on a hi-fidelity amplifier.

Hazell[1] has stated that:

'The most important feature of a tinnitus masking programme is the therapist – who must take a special interest in the tinnitus patients and give them the confidence to persevere with the treatment that many of them initially regard as bizarre and unlikely to succeed. Informal studies in the USA and the UK reveal that success rates in fitting maskers vary from 10 per cent to 85 per cent, and reflect the differences in experience and techniques of masker fitting and patient counselling.'

---

1   Hazell, J.W.P. Management of tinnitus: discussion paper. *Journal of the Royal Society of Medicine 78.* Jan 1986. pp. 56–60.

As Hazell observes at the conclusion of the paper from which the above extract is taken:

> 'For the majority of these people suffering from tinnitus it would seem that masking techniques are likely to be the best available method of management for some years to come.'

5

Hearing Loss is More Than Dull Ears

Most people with normal hearing have little idea of the emotional and behaviourial consequences of hearing loss. An understanding of these consequences is important both for people who suffer hearing loss and for people with normal hearing. First, adjustment is often helped if you know something about the underlying causes of feelings to which you may be prone. Second, a better understanding of the psychological and social consequences of the disability may assist family and friends to give more constructive help. What follows are, of course, generalizations. How you react to a loss of hearing will be influenced by many factors including your personality, the age at which your loss of hearing becomes a disability, and the severity of the loss itself.

Effects on Feelings and Behaviour

A sudden complete or partial loss of hearing is fortunately much less common than a gradual deterioration in aural acuity. A few people are, through disease, accident or other causes, faced with the traumatic experience of having to make a sudden transition from normal hearing to deafness. Far more often the loss of hearing is progressive, and individuals are able to adjust gradually to the limitations. Even in the early stages of progressive hearing loss, however, some behaviourial characteristics may be seen. Although the person may not be regarded as 'deaf', associates may notice such signs as preoccupation, unsociability, absent mindedness, 'living in a world of his own', being 'slow on the uptake' and 'hearing only what he wants to hear'. If and when the hearing loss becomes sufficiently severe to be a practical disability, and especially when it cannot be remedied by surgical or other means, the person concerned is likely to experience both fear and depression.

The fear is usually due to uncertainty about the effect of the hearing loss on a way of life previously taken for granted. Some such effects relating to deafened persons which, depending on the severity of the loss, also relate to those who are hard of hearing, have been identified by McCall[1] as including:

---

[1]   McCall Rosemary. *The Effects of Sudden Profound Hearing Loss in Adult Life.* Paper given to the British Society of Audiology 10 April 1981.

- o The diminished opportunities for conversation and the embarrassment of misunderstandings.
- o Missing the tone of voice which conveys so much.
- o The humiliation of being thought stupid.
- o The impossibilities of easy participation in discussions, groups, meetings, committees, lectures.
- o The depreciation of verbal art and repartee.
- o The fatigue caused by constant alertness – to maintain communication the concentration needed is very demanding.
- o The diminution of social information from which to select, evaluate and formulate opinions and assess the social mood.
- o The inability to do two things at the same time (eat and lipread for example).
- o The reasons for decisions not being clearly understood; being excluded from decision making.

  'I'll tell you afterwards' is no use. 'Afterwards' is too late to participate.

- o The lack of stimulation of discussion and debate; the sharpness of mind on mind.
- o The uncertainty caused when people act unexpectedly without explanations.
- o The enormous difficulties of previously simple encounters. Even a casual request for directions from a passing motorist may be a source of embarrassment.
- o The risk of paranoia feelings and the reality of being left out.

Fear, however, tends to be an initial reaction to hearing loss and diminishes as one adjusts to the disability and learns how to cope successfully with some of the problems. Depression is more persistent. The causes of depression are varied. As explained later in this chapter, depression may result from a sensation of 'deadness'. This feeling has been poignantly described by Lord Ashley who in 1967 was an MP and became totally deaf as a result of a virus infection.

'I sat alone on the terrace (of the Houses of Parliament) watching the Thames. It looked bleak and cold. It was early evening and although I did not expect the river to be busy it seemed exceptionally still – and silent. I thought I had known despair, but now I felt a chill and deeper silence as if part of me was dead.'[2]

When a progressive hearing loss becomes severe or even more so when, as with Lord Ashley, a person is traumatically deafened, the realization of the loss usually gives rise to a sense of bereavement and a period of mourning.

Wright has identified seven symptoms of the 'mourning' reaction to disability:

(1) A sudden and massive constriction of life space.

(2) Unimpaired capacities are ignored.

(3) Pre-occupation with the loss.

(4) Gradual abatement of mourning following a reconstruction of the self concept and body image.

(5) Severity of mourning affected by the values affected by the loss.

(6) Mood of hopelessness, worthlessness.

(7) Perceptions dominated by pre-morbid comparisons with non-disabled persons and the individual's pre-disabled abilities.

Wright believes that the mourning response to disability is necessary for two reasons. First, because there is good reason to believe that the period of mourning can be a healing period during which the wound is first anaesthetized and then gradually closed, leaving the least scaring. Second, because mourning implies a realization of loss and can be the beginning of 'the development of new coping mechanisms for the acquisition of new values which are necessary in the process of overcoming mourning'.

With severe hearing loss the feeling of depression may continue for a prolonged period even after the initial shock reaction to loss has abated. This depression may be accentuated by tinnitus, or the effects of fatigue caused by the energy expended in trying to cope with the demands of an environment in which good hearing is taken for granted.

The emotions of fear and depression may express themselves in outward conduct. An experiment conducted by an American psychologist, Lee Meyerson[3], provides some revealing insights into the ways in which loss of hearing may affect behaviour. He stopped the ears of some volunteers with cotton and wax plugs for a period of 24 hours. Their hearing loss was moderate, about 30 db – insufficient to prevent a tete-a-tete conversation but enough to cause difficulty in hearing speech in a large room. The volunteers were, of course, aware that

---

2   Lord Ashley (1973) *Journey into Silence.* Bodley Head
3   Meyeson, Lee. Experiental Injury: An Approach to the Dynamics of Disability. *Journal of Social Issues,* Vol 4, 1948, pp.68–71.

their 'deafness' was only temporary and that with the removal of the plugs normal hearing would be restored at once. Yet within the short duration of the experiment, a number of characteristic responses to hearing loss were reported.

Some participants stated that they had tried to withdraw from social situations which were perceived as threatening: 'I was conscious of trying to remain aloof so that the girls at the table would ignore me. I felt as if I would like to go out of the house and be alone all day'. 'I pretended to be in a terrible hurry getting ready to leave so I wouldn't have to talk to anyone and maybe not understand what they had said.'

Other volunteers mentioned *aggressive* reactions. One who had experienced difficulty in following a lecture observed: 'The instructor talked in a very low voice. I spent most of the time thinking about how poor a teacher he was, how emotionally maladjusted he must be and calling him every name I could think of'. Sometimes the feelings of aggression were vented on others: 'My wife asked me why I had been so irritable and nasty all day'. Reference was also made to paranoid reactions such as *suspiciousness*: 'I knew they probably weren't but I couldn't help feeling that maybe they were talking about me'. Attempts to conceal the supposed impairment by *bluffing* were reported: 'When they smiled, I smiled. When they laughed, I laughed: the rest of the time I made myself as inconspicuous as possible and prayed for the evening to come to an end.' Some comments revealed that inadequate hearing had resulted in inappropriate behaviour: 'Once I thought the situation was humorous and could not resist a grin. Jane explained later that the girl was very ill and seeking advice whether to go to hospital.'

Two other experiments reported were those of embarrassment arising from misunderstanding conversation and lack of self-confidence in associating with people that had developed into a diffused feeling of uneasiness and restlessness.

The reactions are typical of those experienced by hearing impaired people in real-life situations. Also, a conclusion reached by Meyerson is worth quoting verbatim: 'The psychologically and socially undesirable behaviour that has been reported for physically handicapped persons does not arise because the disabled are different kinds of people but because they have been subjected to different kinds of life experiences.'

Why These Effects Occur

Three possible reasons why impaired hearing may have these effects are: loss of 'affective tone', frustration, and social attitudes to disability.

Loss of Background Noise

An interesting theory about the cause of the depression that often accompanies impaired hearing has been put forward by D.A. Ramsdell (in Hallowell Davies,

Hearing and Deafness). He states that sound is normally perceived simultaneously at three levels, 'primitive', 'warning' and 'symbolic'. The primitive level is the constantly changing pattern of background noise to which we give no attention unless our interest is consciously aroused. Thus, it is only when I stop writing this page and consciously *listen* that I become aware that a bird is singing outside my window, the television is on in another room and a car is passing the house. When we actively respond to auditory signals, as for example footballers to a referee's whistle, we are hearing at the warning level. The most complex level of hearing is the use of sounds as symbols for the purpose of communication, as when we transmit and receive messages in the course of conversation. Ramsdell believes that it is the diminution or loss of hearing at the primitive, rather than the symbolic, level that is responsible for the depressive effects of impaired hearing.

The loss of the sensation of background noise has a twofold effect. First, it is this background noise, or 'affective tone' as it is termed, that makes each of us feel that we belong to our environment. When this tone is lost there is a profound feeling of solitariness and social isolation. One has only to consider how much enjoyment of a football match is heightened by the 'atmosphere' generated by the roaring and singing of the crowd. Second, hearing at the primitive level increases both our sense of security in the present and our ability to cope with future situations. Hearing can warn us of dangers that we cannot see. We may hear footsteps approaching in the dark even though we cannot see the walker. When crossing the road we cannot look in two directions at the same time but, looking left, we can rely on our hearing to warn of traffic coming from the right. Without this auditory alertness it is not surprising that a hearing impaired person feels insecure and uncertain in his environment. Such feelings are strong contributory factors to depression.

Frustration

Frustration arises from the hearing impairment barrier which prevents the attainment of many desirable goals. I may, for example, wish to listen to a lecture given by a famous authority on a subject in which I am interested, but I am frustrated because I cannot hear what he has to say. Nor can I keep pace with office or family conversations.

Reactions to frustration may be either positive or negative. Positive reactions include problem solving, accepting substitute goals and finding a compensation. One common negative response is that of *aggression*, which can take three main forms.

It can be physical, as when a direct attack is made on the barrier that causes the frustration. Aggression may, of course, also be positive – as when, through a surgeon, we attack the bony growth that prevents the movement of the stapes in otosclerosis. Aggression may be verbal, when we relieve pent-up frustration by cursing the loss of hearing that prevents the attainment of so many goals. There is also substitute aggression in which a person vents all his tension on his family and friends. It will be recalled that one of Meyerson's volunteers reported 'my wife asked me why I had been so irritable and nasty all day'. An understanding of the causes of this substitute aggression may make it easier to live with a hearing impaired person and improve the quality of his personal relationships.

Other negative reactions which may afflict a person with a loss of hearing are those of regression, fixation, withdrawal and resignation. We *regress* when we engage in childish forms of behaviour such as weeping or temper tantrums. *Fixation* is a compulsion to continue with a type of behaviour that will accomplish nothing towards the removal of the frustrating barrier. Sadly, people who have been advised by a competent otologist that nothing can be done to cure the hearing loss will often continue to visit other ear specialists in the vain hope that one will have some remedy unknown to the others. Worse still, they go to quacks and charlatans who have no qualms about prescribing useless and expensive appliances or courses of treatment. *Withdrawal* has already been noted as a response which may be adopted by a person who finds that interaction with the hearing world imposes too great a strain. *Resignation* may be the end result of prolonged frustration; the individual no longer seeks constructive ways of dealing with his or her disability and gives up, lapsing eventually into apathy and despair.

Social Attitudes

The attitudes of a person with impaired hearing are only partially derived from the actual handicap. They are also affected by the social attitudes shown by non-handicapped people. A disabled person may come to accept the attitudes he has encountered from society as his own.

Two sociological terms that help us to understand social attitudes to hearing impairment are 'deviance' and 'stigma'. Deviant behaviour violates the generally accepted norms of society. It is generally assumed that we live in a hearing world and that normal people are hearing people. We take it for granted that if a person is spoken to he will make an appropriate reply, that he will take evasive action if we sound our car horn and that he will respond to the telephone or door bell. When a hearing-impaired person deviates from such norms, his handicap will be seen as something discreditable. He will become aware of this 'stigma' when an employer turns him down or people with normal hearing tend to adopt a superior role or to display pity or impatience. The stigma is accentuated by the general tendency to label everyone with a hearing loss as 'deaf', irrespective of its extent or time of onset. There is also an unfortunate belief that in some ways deafness is related to daftness; too often the deaf and hard of hearing are stereotyped as slow-thinking and deficient in intelligence. Deafness, unlike blindness, is not a disability that makes an instinctive appeal to human sympathy. It is significant that while the deaf are usually found in comedies the blind appear in tragedies!

E. Goffman in *Stigma – Notes on the Management of Spoiled Identity* [4] has stated that the rewards of being considered normal are so great that all handicapped people in a position to do so will, on occasion, attempt to bluff that they are 'normal'. Since, unlike persons who are blind or physically disabled, these who are hearing impaired display no external symptoms, there is a strong temptation to resort to subterfuges. Frances Warfield has given some amusing examples (in *There's No Need to Shout*) of the covers she adopted at football games to disguise the fact that she was hard of hearing: 'be chilly and muffle ears comically in scarf and lap robe; have foot go to sleep and create noise and laughter by stamping; divert escort's attention to getting and consuming of hot dogs, etc; do tricks with matches or handkerchiefs and encourage escort to do the same, tear up programmes; make and sail paper darts.' And at dances, she suggests: 'continue to sing tune last played; ask to be shown new dance step; play cagey and pretend you won't answer questions – you know the answer but you're not telling; read your partner's palm; powder your nose; lose something; remember you have to go the telephone; ask for some punch'.

This desire to pass as normal also explains the reluctance of many hard of hearing people to wear a hearing aid; they regard it as a stigma symbol advertising their disability. The wish for concealment is, of course, recognized by the hearing aid manufacturers, both at the design stage when some efficiency in performance may be sacrificed in the interest of making the aid as small as possible, and in advertising when stress is laid on the aid's inconspicuousness. In short, bluffing is a desperate attempt by an individual threatened with being, or being thought, abnormal to retain the status and acceptability of a 'normal' person. When bluffing is no longer possible, or the strain of keeping up the pretence of normality becomes too great, the hearing impaired person will tend to resort to withdrawal from society.

Coping with the Emotional Effects

It is easier to write about the effects of hearing impairment on personality and behaviour, and their causes, than to suggest just how they may be avoided or overcome. Your adjustment, or your friend's or relative's adjustment, to loss of

---

4   Goffman, E. (1963) *Stigma – Notes on the Management of Spoiled Identity*. London: Pelican.

hearing depends not only on the cause, severity and expected progress of the disability, but also on such variables as age, intelligence, personality, education and support received from family, friends and employers. In making suggestions as how to cope, it is impossible to avoid generalizations. There is also the danger that a reader, facing the harsh reality of impaired hearing, may dismiss such generalizations as platitudinous preaching. The answer to that charge is that what follows is based not on idle theorizing but on the writer's twenty years' personal experience of hearing impairment. This experience led to the conclusion that if one is to modify the emotional and behaviourial effects of hearing loss it is necessary to cultivate at least five virtues: knowledge, honesty, empathy, activity and courage.

Knowledge

The fact that one's ears are dull is no reason why one's mind should not be active. A hearing impaired person should try to discover, through reading and conversation with others, as much as possible about his disability and the procedures, devices and agencies that may exist for its relief.

At the simplest level such information will make him aware of such gadgets as the flashing door bells and other devices mentioned in Chapter 6. Knowledge about the possible results of hearing loss on behaviour can also prevent some embarrassing situations. For example, people with a conductive loss tend to speak softly; those with a sensorineural loss are prone to shout. Knowing this simple fact will enable a person to modulate his voice appropriately. Being aware that 'substitute aggression' is a negative response to frustration may help an individual to curb any tendency to relieve his tension by venting his frustrations on others. Knowledge enables the person with a disability to evaluate information and an informed person is much less likely to be taken in by charlatans offering wonder-cures. The very fact that you are reading this page indicates a desire to know something about hearing impairment. This attitude of curiosity and desire for understanding should be maintained.

Honesty

Honesty in this context means a firm resolve to avoid bluffing. No hearing impaired person can bluff for very long, and even the attempt may make him or her appear ridiculous and involve unnecessary strain. Most people will be too polite to tell him that they are aware of his impairment and will allow him to believe that the bluff is succeeding when, in fact, he is fooling no one. It is much better to admit to a disability at the outset.

If you cannot hear what is being said, the sensible thing is to explain simply and courteously that you don't hear well. The vast majority of people will then do all they can to help, and the minority who are impatient or ignorant can usually be ignored.

Most hearing impaired people are more self-conscious than they need be. This point can be illustrated by a personal experience. After the first of two successful stapedectomy operations the writer returned to work and proudly asked a number of colleagues 'do you notice anything different?', expecting them to say at once 'You're not wearing your hearing aid.' To his surprise they scrutinized him closely and then admitted that they could not detect anything unusual. They had long since ceased even to notice the hearing aid which the writer had thought to be so conspicuous.

Empathy

Empathy is the ability to identify with others. Empathy helps in making allowance for any conduct and attitudes from others that arise from ignorance and misunderstanding. Thus, at the beginning of this chapter it was stated that few people with normal ears are aware of the emotional and behavioural consequences of impaired hearing. It is also true that some people shy away from all types of disability because they are embarrassed and uncertain what to do. In such cases, empathy enables the person with a disability to take the initiative and put the non-disabled at ease by informing them how they can best assist. A person with a severe hearing loss might explain 'there is no need to shout, but if you will face the light and speak slowly I shall probably understand what you are saying'. Empathy leads to the realization that even the most patient husband or wife will also experience strain from having to act as a second pair of ears for a partner with defective hearing. It is all too easy for a hard-of-hearing person to become so full of self-pity that he is oblivious to the needs, difficulties and rights of others. A television set turned on at full volume can turn a home into a hell for everyone else there. A hearing impaired person has to try to extend the same understanding to others that he expects to receive.

Activity

The best method of counteracting depression and social isolation is to cultivate some physical or mental activity. It may be mentioned here that constructive activity such as can be obtained from a hobby or work can divert the mind away from the disability and thereby prevent the introspection that so often results in depression.

Courage

Alfred Adler, the great Viennese psychologist, maintained that physical defects, whether congenital or acquired, invariably result in feelings of inferiority. These feelings, which often arise from the reduced ability of the disabled person to compete and interact with the non-disabled, may also be reinforced by social attitudes. Unless a disabled person is alert to the possibility he tends to become what he is expected to be. A person who, because of his impaired hearing, is regarded by his family and associates as dull and slow may come to regard these valuations as true. He will gradually develop an inferiority complex and fatalistically resign himself to a crippling situation which he will make no attempt to correct or improve. He may even attempt to exploit his ascribed inferiority to claim attention or gain sympathy. Aggression, self-assertion and rebellion may also be negative responses to inferiority.

A more constructive approach to overcoming inferiority is to find a compensation. Compensation involves finding out what can be done well and doing it. Thus a hearing impaired person can compensate for any feeling of inferiority by channelling his energies into some activity that provides scope for demonstrating competence. For Adler the decisive factor in determining whether an individual would succumb to or overcome inferiority was courage:

> 'By courage and training disabilities may be so compensated that they even become great abilities. When correctly encountered a disability becomes a stimulus that impels towards a higher achievement... Those who have attained remarkable success in life have often been handicapped in the beginning with disabilities and with great feelings of inferiority. On the other hand we find that a person who believes himself to be the victim of inherited deficiencies and disabilities lessens his efforts with a consequent feeling of hopelessness. His development is thus permanently retarded.' (Adler)[5]

Of the three possible attitudes to hearing impairment – rebellion, resignation and redemption – it is only the latter that, like Wordsworth's Happy Warrior, 'turns necessity to glorious gain' and yields positive results. Two quotations may be a source of inspiration. The first states that 'character is a measure of the things that one has overcome'.

The second is a prayer by Reinhold Niebuhr:

> 'God give me the serenity to accept the things I cannot change, the courage to change the things I can, and the wisdom to know the difference.'

---

5   Adler, Alfred. *Problems of Neurosis.*

6
Hearing Aids and Other Devices

The oldest, simplest and most readily accessible aid to hearing is the cupped hand behind the ear. By channelling more energy into the ear via the cupped hand sound level at the ear can be raised by about 7 decibels.

The *acoustic fan* shown in Figure 6.1 is one of many ingenious devices which were available to provide inconspicuous assistance to people with impaired hearing.

Figure 6.1. Acoustic Fan

Historic hearing devices have been classified into such groups as:

(1) Speaking tubes.

(2) Ear trumpets.

(3) Concealed or camouflaged sound receptors, for example acoustic chairs, fans, hats, hair combs, walking sticks and so forth.

(4) Devices to increase the size and capacity of parts of the sound-conducting mechanism, for example artificial external ears (auricles) and artificial ear drums.

(5) Non-electric bone conduction devices, for example strips of wood, metal or vulcanite to conduct sound through the skull.

Some of the appliances marketed were quite valueless, and even attempted to exploit a desperate desire by hard of hearing people to hear as inconspicuously as possible. However, speaking tubes and ear trumpets rendered real assistance and are still used by some elderly people who find difficulty in adapting to electronic aids (see conversation aids later in the chapter). It is possible to make a speaking tube at very little cost by purchasing about 3 ft or 10mm bore rubber tube from a chemist and pushing a small plastic or metal funnel into one end for speaking into.

It is, however, the electronic hearing aid that most people think about when considering how they can compensate for hearing loss. Although Alexander Graham Bell was seeking to make an electric hearing aid for his wife when, in 1876, he invented the telephone, it was not until 1898 that such an instrument was first marketed in America by the Dictograph Company.

The early electric hearing aids were very cumbersome. The *Acousticon* shown in Figure 6.2 comprised a microphone, a battery and a disc earphone was described in the early days of the twentieth century as *'the most perfect of the numberless attempts made to aid the deaf by electrical means.'*

The gradual reduction in the size of electronic hearing aids was encouraged first by the development of miniature radio valves and then by transistors. It has, however, been the application of microchip technology that has made possible the small, inconspicuous and highly efficient hearing aids currently available.

This chapter attempts to describe the construction and types of hearing aids, and how they can be acquired, used and maintained. Reference is also made to other devices that may help a hearing impaired person to cope with the demands of daily living.

Figure 6.2. The Acousticon

The Components of a Hearing Aid

Essentially, a hearing aid is an amplifying device. As shown in Figure 6.3 it has four main components: a microphone, an amplifier, a receiver, a power supply. A separate ear mould is an important factor in its efficiency where the system is modular.

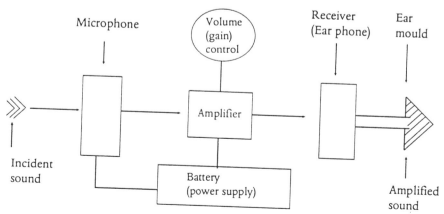

Figure 6.3. The Components of a Hearing Aid System

The Microphone

The purpose of the microphone is to convert energy carried by the sound waves into electrical energy. This is done by means of a diaphragm which is made to vibrate by the sound waves, very much like the ear drum in the human ear.

The Amplifier

An amplifier can be defined as a device for increasing the energy of a circuit. The amplifier, therefore, has the function of increasing the electrical voltage received by the microphone or, in other words, to deliver a high energy output in relation to a small energy input. Amplifiers comprise a complicated assortment of transistors, capacitors and resistors that it would be impracticable to attempt to describe here. Today's amplifier is usually constructed via *chip technology*.

The Receiver

The receiver reverses the function of the microphone. Where the microphone changes sound waves into electrical energy the receiver transduces the electrical energy back into sound waves. *Receivers* feed sound into the ear canal by means of an ear mould. Where there is ear discharge or a very significant air-bone audiometric gap, a *bone conduction* receiver may be fitted. A bone conduction receiver is essentially a vibrator which is placed against the mastoid so that sound can be transmitted to the inner ear. The disadvantage of bone conduction receivers, which are limited to body and spectacle aids, is that since bone is a high impedance medium, more energy, with a consequent increase in battery consumption, is required. Bone conduction receivers transmit a narrower range of frequencies and, with body aids, a headband must be worn to ensure an adequate amount of pressure on the mastoid. Unless properly fitted, this may cause discomfort.

The Power Supply

The battery is the heart of the hearing aid since it provides the power. Apart from 1.5 volt alkaline manganese 'penlite' batteries used for body worn aids, hearing aid batteries are generally of button cell construction and come in a variety of miniature sizes. Currently most operate on the principle of zinc-air construction. Zinc-air batteries last twice as long as mercury batteries, which they have largely replaced, and are also more acceptable since mercury batteries are a source of environmental pollution.

The four currently most popular battery sizes are 10 (or 230), 312, 13 and 675. The actual sizes are shown in Figure 6.4. Even smaller batteries are likely to be introduced in the near future.

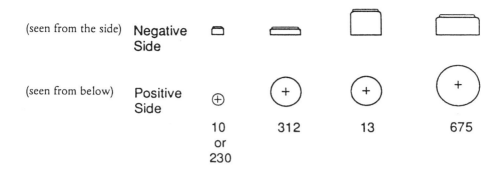

Figure 6.4. Hearing Aid Actual Battery Sizes

As can be seen the positive (+) side of the battery is stamped on the underside. The negative side is the raised circle.

You should note the following important points regarding batteries:

o Hearing aids do not require the use of batteries from any particular manufacturer. Provided that the battery has the appropriate number it is interchangeable even though the letters, which are used by the manufacturer for identification purposes, are different.

o If you insert the battery incorrectly, the battery drawer will not close, or the instrument will not function.

o Always store batteries in cool, dry conditions.

o Take batteries out of hearing aids which are not in regular use.

o Keep battery contacts clean; remove any deposit with a dry cloth.

o Never throw batteries in the fire.

o Keep batteries away from children and pets; always dispose of them safely.

The Ear Mould and Tubing

These individual prosthetic components extend beyond the earphone outlet and are often referred to as *the plumbing*. They are important.

Ear moulds

Ear moulds are designed to fit the contours of the ear and are usually made from hard or soft acrylic but there are a number of alternative materials which have merits. Soft vinyl, for example, may be more comfortable and provide a better seal but can be less durable and cannot be used for certain ear mould types.

The ear mould has three functions. The first function is to provide, together with the tubing, where applicable, a medium through which sound travels from the receiver to the user's ear drum without leakage which causes feedback or *whistling*. Second, the ear mould can acoustically *shape* a signal once it has been transduced by the receiver. Third, the ear mould acts as an anchor to keep the aid firmly attached to the ear.

There are a number of ear mould styles. The selection of a particular style by the dispenser is usually determined by such criteria as the type of aid, the possibility of acoustic feedback, the degree of hearing loss and the comfort of the user. Some styles of ear moulds include

> *Regular* moulds, utilized only on body aids. These are solid moulds with a snap ring to accommodate an appropriate receiver.
>
> *Shell* moulds, used with behind-the-ear aids, are similar to 'shells' except that the centre of the concha bowl is removed, leaving a frame around the 'concha' for retention.
>
> *Half-shell* moulds used with behind-the-ear and in-the-ear aids only cover the bottom depth of the concha.
>
> *Canal* moulds are also used for behind-the-ear and in-the-ear aids and are popular because they are inconspicuous and easy to insert. They are, however, less secure in the ear and may create feedback at high volume when more acoustic gain is required.

The effect of the ear mould on an aid's low-frequency response may also be altered by drilling a hole or *vent* either parallel or diagonal to the mould's sound output channel, thus intentionally producing a sound leak. 'Venting' of moulds is undertaken for several reasons: to improve sound quality, to relieve the feeling of fullness in the ear experienced by some aid users and to enhance high frequency responses by attenuating or diminishing the lows. The main problem with venting can be the enhancement of feedback on the escape of amplified sound.

The Tubing

The *tubing* from the receiver to the ear mould can, according to the length an diameter, affect the response of your aid. An increase or decrease in the internal diameter of the tubing can have a corresponding effect on mid or high frequency gain and output. substituting the constant bore tubing with a tube in which the internal diameter increases as it nears the ear canal can enhance high frequency response. This is known as the *horn* effect. Conversely a *reverse horn effect* in which the tubing diameter is reduced has the effect of impeding high frequency transmission.

Hearing Aid Features

Hearing aid dispensers can sometimes over-emphasize the special features of their instrument. To avoid being blinded with science you should be able to recognize the names of some of these features and know what they are designed to do.

The Volume Control (VC)

This control is more accurately called the *gain control* since it controls amplification (gain) rather than loudness. Gain is the output of the aid at the receiver minus the output at the microphone – expressed in decibels. If the output of an aid is given as 100 dB with the input 60 dB, then at the given frequency the gain would be 40 dB. The gain control is usually a small wheel that can be moved to regulate the amplifier's output according to the needs of the user or the amount of background noise.

Automatic Gain Control (AGC)

Excessively loud sounds can cause discomfort and even pain to the wearer of an aid. The function of an AGC is to limit the maximum output of the amplifier so that, irrespective of the input level, the output level can never exceed a predetermined volume which is below the user's pain threshold or uncomfortable loudness level.

Peak Clipping (PC)

Like AGC this is a method of limiting the maximum output of the amplifier. As we have seen, the intensity of a sound wave when converted into electrical energy by the receiver can be considered to be represented by its amplitude or height. Peak clipping cuts off peak intensities whenever they exceed a preset limit. The loss in speech intelligibility when peak intensities are not transmitted by an aid is insignificant. Nearly all aids have some form of peak clipping.

Dynamic Range Compression (DRC)

Like AGC and peak clipping, DRC is intended to control sound pressures to a level below that at which discomfort and distortion is experienced. Unlike AGC and PC which are limited to a fixed *output* sound pressure, DRC is linked to a fixed *input* sound pressure level. DRC is particularly useful in cases of sensorineural impairment when recruitment is pronounced.

Tone Control (TC)

This is a control designed to make sound clearer by modifying either the high or low frequencies. If the switch is set in the 'high' position, less amplification will be given to the low and mid-frequencies. In 'low' position, the high frequencies will be reduced.

Telecoil or T-Switch

A T-switch enables an aid to respond to magnetic fields rather than sound. When the switch is in the T (telephone) position, the microphone is automatically disconnected and only the pickup-coil is operative. The T-switch, therefore, enables the user to listen to the telephone or television exclusively, with extraneous background noise eliminated. All public telephones have an induction coupler. Many public places such as theatres and churches have installed induction loop systems. Where such systems are present (symbolized by a logo of the ear) you can, by using the T-switch to bypass the microphone of your aid, tune directly into the sound you wish to hear. Some hearing aids have an MT switch which allows the microphone and telecoil to be active at the same time the 'M' switch giving normal reception.

Programme Aids

Most aids have screw-set controls (potentiometric) which enable the dispenser to fine tune the instrument in respect of gain and tone by means of a small screwdriver. Increasingly, however, programmable aids are being developed by which the different compression channels are dispenser selected and set to allow the aid to adapt to different listening situations such as a quiet conversation at home, orchestral music and communicating at a party.

Apart from the ability to adjust to different sound conditions either automatically or by a remote control device, programmable aids have other advantages. These include:

○ precision of electroacoustic adjustment at the time of fitting

○ ability to adjust gain and output to meet subsequent changes in hearing loss

○ automatic signal processing strategies not available with non-programmable instruments.

Although it has been estimated that up to 80 per cent of hearing aid users can benefit from programmable aids, such aids may not be approved for:

○ severe profound losses. Stronger gain behind-the-ear (BTE) and in-the-ear (ITE) aids are, however, in the course of development.

○ where there is normal hearing in the 2000–3000 hZ frequency range. Programmable aids are most beneficial for low and mid frequencies. The advantages of programmability are reduced when little or no gain in these frequencies is required.

○ CROS or BICROS (see below, *msp 140*) fittings. Non-programmable aids are currently the only choice if a wireless CROS or BICROS fitting is required.

When contemplating a programmable aid it is useful to ask the following questions:

- How many channels has the aid? Many programmable aids have only one channel. Other, generally more expensive aids, have up to three (or more) channels.
- How many memories/situations has the aid. These can vary from one to ten although most aids have two to four.
- Does the aid adjust automatically to different sound situations or have a remote control device?

Programmable aids are now available from all the leading hearing aid manufacturers.

Type of Hearing Aids

Although the primary components are the same, electronic aids for personal use are available in an extensive variety of makes, shapes and models. Apart from cochlea implants, which are significantly different from conventional instruments, personal hearing aids can be categorized into six main types.

1. Body Aids

With these aids the microphone, amplifier, batteries and controls are located in a case which is attached to the user's clothing. A cord links the case to the receiver which clips into a solid ear mould.

A Y-shaped cord can be used to deliver sound to both ears. This arrangement, however, does not permit each ear to function independently and is not therefore a true binaural fitting. Body aids have certain advantages, particularly for severely or profoundly hearing impaired persons since the physical separation of the microphone from the receiver allows high gain without acoustic feedback. Body aids are also suitable for people who have manual dexterity problems including some very young and very old users.

Apart from being bulkier than behind and in-the-ear aids, body aids are susceptible to 'clothes rub', the noise caused by the rubbing of the user's clothes against the microphone. Localization of sound with a body aid is also impossible.

2. In the Ear (ITE) Aids

These are currently the most popular hearing aids. With ITE aids all the components are housed in the shell of the aid itself so that the need for a connecting wire or tube to the ear mould is avoided.

ITE aids are of two types. Full shell aids fill the entire concha of the ear. In the canal (ITC) aids fit in the ear canal either near the entrance or well down, in which case they are termed deep canal models. The further down the microphone is positioned, the greater can be the improvement in sound intensity and reception.

Clearly the shell of the aid will have to be contoured to the shape of the concha or ear passage of the user and for this reason ITE aids are sometimes referred to as 'custom' hearing aids. ITE aids are ideal for binaural applications, in part because they restore a sense of spatial perception. ITE aids are rarely recommended for very severe or profound hearing losses, although recent advances in technology make them suitable for a very wide range of hearing impairments. Although some users have difficulty in manipulating the small controls, others find that having everything in the one piece actually makes the aid easier to handle.

3. Behind the Ear (BTE) Aids

As the name implies all the components of a BTE aid are contained in a small case worn behind the ear. A tube leads to the ear mould which anchors the aid in the ear. Binaural hearing can be obtained by the use of two aids in which the microphone of each preferably faces forward. Quality BTEs, which are larger than ITEs, can deliver superior performance simply as they can house more technology. They can, for example, enhance speech clarity even in background noise and amplify soft sounds without distorting the louder sounds. The audiological requirements for nearly any user can be achieved so that BTE aids can assist even in the cases of very complex hearing impairments.

4. Spectacle Hearing Aids

These have the microphone, amplifier and receiver located in either one or both spectacle arms. As with a BTE aid, an ear mould and tubing carry the sound to the ear. Binaural hearing can be provided if both ears are utilized. These aids have advantages for the users of both spectacle and hearing aids. They can also be easily adapted for CROS aids (see below). Spectacle aids can, however, be inconvenient. To change a battery, for example, the spectacles must be taken off; if the aid requires repairs the user is temporarily bereft of both assisted sight and hearing. For these reasons spectacle aids have lost some of their popularity. Some manufacturers do, however, provide arms that enable BTE aids to be attached to spectacles. For the reasons stated such attachments are often preferable.

5. Bone Conduction (BC) Aids

As explained above, the principal difference between air and bone conduction aids is the receiver. With bone conduction aids the receiver is essentially a vibrator placed against the mastoid so that sound can be transmitted into the inner ear. BC aids are in fact rarely prescribed today except for users with conductive hearing impairments who, for some reason, cannot have the ear canal occluded by an ear mould.

6. CROS Aids

If you have one 'good ear' and one 'bad ear' which cannot be helped by a monaural aid you will have difficulty at parties or committee meetings in hearing what people located on your 'bad' side are saying. A CROS aid can be the solution for this difficulty CROS stands for *Contralateral Routing of Signal* or the sending of sound from one side of the head to the other. Essentially a CROS aid sends sound from a microphone placed on the bad side to a receiver in the 'good ear'. The acronym BICROS is used where there is some hearing loss in the good ear for which amplification is required. With BICROS, two microphones are fed into a mixer unit that combines them before amplifying and transmitting them into the usable ear. CROS and BICROS, therefore, provide a form of binaural hearing. CROS aids may be BTE, Spectacle or ITE models. As shown by the table, Figure 6.5, some hearing aid users have special needs that may restrict the style of hearing aid chosen.

Developments in Hearing Aids

Hearing aids are rapidly improving in performance and features whilst also becoming smaller and cosmetically more attractive. At the time of writing (1995) significant developments are being made, particularly in the fields of frequency selectivity, automatic gain control and suppression of acoustic feedback.

Frequency selectivity is the ability to separate out individual frequencies in complex sounds and is vital to understanding speech, particularly in background noise. Work is in progress aimed at boosting those parts of the noise spectrum attributable to speech while suppressing those attributable to noise, thereby giving an effective improvement in speech to noise ratios.

In the area of automatic gain control (AGC), researchers at Cambridge are concerned with the development of a prototype and with three separate forms of AGC: the first will enable the user to move without discomfort from a quiet to noisy environment without the need to adjust the aid's controls; the second will 'protect' the user from sudden intense sounds such as the slamming of a door; the third will assist the user to hear weaker speech sounds such as 'p' or 'r'.

Research is also in progress into incorporating an adaptive suppression system into a normal size power BTE instrument that will provide a more effective approach to feedback or 'whistling' due to the escape of amplified sound from the ear canal into the microphone of the hearing aid.

Other areas under review include multi-microphone technology and the further development of deep canal aids.

Style of Aid	Appropriate Hearing Loss	Comments
Body Aid	1 Severe-Profound Losses	1 User who is confined to bed
		2 User who requires large controls
		3 May be adapted with bone conduction receiver for bone-conduction aid
ITE Aid	1 Mild-severe loss	1 May be adapted for CROS or BICROS
	2 Any configuration of loss	2 May be easier to handle than BTE because of single piece
	3 Special circuitry available	
ITC Aid	1 Mild-severe loss	1 Most cosmetically appealing
	2 Special circuitry available	
BTE Aid	1 Any degree of loss	1 May be adapted for CROS or BICROS
	2 Any configuration of loss	2 User who requires larger controls than ITE aid
	3 Special circuitry available, ie audiological flexibility	
Spectacle Aid	1 Moderate-severe loss	1 May be adapted for CROS or BICROS
		2 May be adapted for bone conduction fitting

Figure 6.5
Courtesy Starkey Technical Services Ltd

The National Health Aid and How to Get One

Due to the advocacy of the then Duke of Montrose who, at the time was President of the RNID, hearing aids were included among the appliances which can be issued on free loan under the provisions of the 1946 National Health Service Act.

At the time of writing the NHS provides a range of behind-the-ear aids in four series known as BE 10, BE 20, BE 30 and BE 50, catering respectively for moderate, moderate to severe and severe to profound hearing losses. There are also the BW 80 body worn aids for severe to profound losses. These BW aids can also be used with a bone conductor. It is, however, likely that these series classifications will be gradually phased out.

The first step in obtaining an NHS aid is to discuss the matter with your General Practitioner. If the GP agrees that you would benefit from an aid the subsequent procedure may be along traditional or direct referral lines.

Under the traditional (TR) system the GP will refer you to a hospital-based ear nose and throat (ENT) consultant or audiological physician. You will then receive an ENT examination as a check on the cause of your hearing impairment and possible alternative treatment. This will normally be followed by a visit to the hospital audiological unit (or Hearing Aid Centre) where you may undergo further audiological tests which will determine which of the available range of NHS aids is most appropriate for your loss. Finally an impression will be sent away to have an ear mould made from it. When the hospital receives the ear mould it will recall you to the Hearing Aid Centre where you will be fitted with the aid and instructed in its use. Many Centres will ask you to return in one to three months' time so that your progress with the aid can be reviewed. You may also be referred for further help with your hearing problem to a hearing therapist or social worker.

The direct referral (DR) procedure was recommended by the RNID in their 1988 publication *Hearing Aids – the Case for Change* as a means of reducing waiting times by removing a significant proportion of patients from ENT waiting lists, thus speeding up the processes of dispensing aids and providing treatment. The DR procedure is exactly the same as for the TR procedure except that GPs refer appropriate patients directly to the Hearing Aid Centre. The GP is expected to ensure that DR patients show no signs of significant ear abnormalities. At the Hearing Aid Clinic you will be examined by an audiological technician who will use a set of guidelines to identify potential medical conditions. Should such conditions be detected you will be referred to the ENT Department.

A report on the two methods, *Direct Referral Systems for Hearing Aid Provision*, prepared for the Department of Health identified five areas for the evaluation of DR schemes namely: waiting times, safety, quality assurance, staff satisfaction and cost effectiveness. From the patient's viewpoint, the most important are waiting times, safety and quality assurance. The survey indicated that under the DR system, waiting times are substantially reduced. While the risk that a potentially serious condition might be overlooked is greater under the DR system, it is in fact insignificant. In the survey the rate of potentially serious technician management failures was about one in every 156 patients. Because of the high power output of NHS BW 80 aids with the possibility of damage to residual hearing, these instruments may only be fitted on the specific recommendation of a consultant otologist or consultant in audiological medicine.

Patient satisfaction with DR schemes was very high. Overall, 84 per cent of DR patients made positive statements about the service compared with 59 per cent of TR patients.

Other aspects of NHS provision are important.

First, all NHS aids are *lent* not given and if for nay reason an instrument is no longer required it should be returned to the Hearing Aid Centre without delay.

Second, Hearing Aid Centres repair or replace aids free of charge although, theoretically, a charge can be made if a replacement is needed due to your carelessness or maltreatment. Replacement batteries are also supplied free.

Third, although most patients in need of a hearing aid will be able to benefit from one of the models in the NHS range, a consultant otologist has a discretion to prescribe alternative models when he or she considers that '*an adult young person or child requires an aid outside the NHS range*'.

Fourth, a consultant or audiological technician may provide two aids where both ears are in fact available.

Finally, in September 1994, the Department of Health announced that suitably qualified, private practice hearing aid dispensers are eligible for employment as Medical Technical Officers in the NHS. A number of Health Authorities and Audiology Departments operate private hearing aid centres, thus enabling patients to choose between a 'free' NHS aid or a privately purchased aid.

Hearing Therapists

In 1976 a Report on the Rehabilitation of the Adult Hearing Impaired issued by the DHSS Advisory Committee on Services for the Hearing Impaired recommended that a new class of worker known as a hearing therapist should be created within the NHS. The recommendation led to the establishment of a one-year training course at the City Lit Centre for Deaf People and Speech Therapy, London. In 1994 a course of post-graduate professional training for appropriately qualified individuals wishing to specialize as hearing therapists was contemplated Manchester University. This development has not at the time of writing (1995) materialised.

The first hearing therapists took up their appointments in 1979. Currently (1995) about 80 therapists are in post, mainly at major hospitals in the UK. This is far below the estimated figure of 300 therapists required to provide an adequate service. The Society of Hearing Therapists represents the interests of the profession.

The range of activities of the Hearing Therapist who works as a member of a multi-disciplinary team which includes clinical, technical and social work staff is shown in Figure 6.6.

Briefly, the role of the hearing therapist is to help individuals with an *acquired* hearing loss to make the most of their residual hearing. A tailor-made programme is therefore planned for each patient which includes help with the hearing aid, lip reading instruction, auditory training, advice about environmental aids and suggestions for creating more favourable conditions for using lipreading. The principle is that only by enabling hearing impaired individuals to make use of

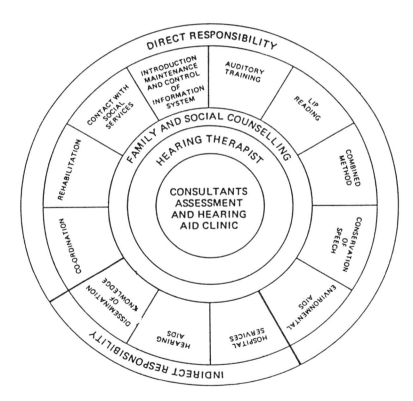

Figure 6.6. Direct and indirect responsibilities of the hearing therapist

every available visual and auditory clue can their ability to live in a world of sound with less anxiety be enhanced. Problems concerning home, work and social occasions are also discussed and advice given that may alleviate the stress of living with a hearing loss. As the Society has well stated: '*Good aural rehabilitation given at the right time can prevent a hearing impairment from becoming a serious handicap.*'

Privately Dispensed Hearing Aids

It has been estimated that about 20 per cent of UK hearing aid users have commercial or privately dispensed aids. While the comprehensive range of NHS aids is capable of meeting the needs of most people with moderate to profound hearing losses, a private aid has certain advantages that may justify the cost:

- Most NHS aids currently available are behind-the-ear and body worn aids, although some in-the-ear models are becoming available through the NHS. If you want an in-the-canal (ITC), a spectacle or a CROS or BICROS aid you will have to purchase privately.

- A private aid can be programmed to meet the requirements of your individual hearing loss. The NHS aid will be the model which, in the opinion of the centre staff, most closely approximates to your loss. The analogy is the difference between an 'off the peg' and a 'tailor-made' suit. Even with a private aid, however, you must not expect the hearing aid dispenser to prescribe with the same precision as an optician.

- Privately supplied aids may incorporate features not available with NHS aids such as multi-channel programmes enabling you to adapt the aid to several different hearing environments, for example a quiet room, a noisy street, music or a party where speech discrimination may be difficult. There is, of course, no reason why you should not have both an NHS and a commercial aid.

The Hearing Aid Council and Advertising Standards Authority

Hearing aid dispensers and persons employing such dispensers are required to adhere to the Code of Practice of the Hearing Aid Council.

The Hearing Aid Council was established by the Board of Trade in 1969 following the passing in the previous year of the Hearing Aid Council Act. The main statutory responsibilities of the Council are:

(1) To provide for the registration with the Council of all dispensers selling hearing aids and all employees of such dispensers. It is now illegal for unregistered individuals, partnerships or companies to sell hearing aids.

The Disciplinary Committee of the Council has power to remove the name of any registered person or body corporate from the register.

(2) To lay down Standards of Competence for hearing aid dispensers and those wishing to take up the occupation.

(3) To lay down a Code of Practice for adoption by the registered dispensers and employers of dispensers. This Code is reproduced in *Appendix 1*.

When introducing the Hearing Aid Council Bill in 1968, Laurie Pavitt declared that his purpose was '*to protect the hard of hearing from the hard selling*' and to put service, education and information in the place of gimmicky sales promotion. There is little doubt that the Act, with the cooperation of the hearing aid industry, has done much to achieve these aims.

The Hearing Aid Council, however, has no jurisdiction over hearing aid advertisements. The only legal remedy against mis-statements is in the Trades Description Act. The Advertising Standards Authority has published the British Code of Advertising Practice which lays down the following rules for advertisements relating to hearing aids and hearing aid exhibitions.

Hearing Aids

(1) No advertisement for a hearing aid should make any claim which goes beyond suggesting that an aid can offer assistance in enabling the user to have clearer, or sharper, hearing ability. In particular there should be no claim that an aid can restore natural hearing, ie the normal acuity of perception enjoyed earlier in life by the prospective purchaser.

(2) Advertisements addressed to sections of the public such as old age pensioners should not give the impression that all those who fall into the category necessarily require hearing aids or will benefit from their use.

(3) No impression should be given in any advertisement that a particular aid is suitable for all potential users.

(4) Where it is not otherwise readily apparent, advertisements should clearly explain how or where an aid is worn, and in simple terms, how it operates.

(5) Any claims for novelty of action, or development in hearing aid technology require detailed substantiation.

(6) When a hearing aid exhibition is commercially promoted, that fact should be clearly apparent from any advertisement for it and the full name and address of the advertiser's head office should be prominently stated.

(7) Advertisers should have regard generally to the requirements of the Hearing Aid Council's Code of Practice, and in particular to Item 10 of that Code which provides guidance on home visits.

If you have a complaint against a hearing aid dispenser, or consider that you have been misled by an advertisement, the initial move is to take up the complaint personally or in writing with the dispenser or his/her employer. If you fail to obtain satisfaction, report the circumstances with *copies* of supporting evidence to the Hearing Aid Council or Advertising Standards Authority, whichever is appropriate. If the matter is still not resolved, the only course is to seek legal remedies – not a thing to do lightly and without sound professional advice.

Buying a Privately Dispensed Hearing Aid

It is not difficult to find a hearing aid dispenser. The Yellow Pages telephone directory provides a list of such dispensers. It is wise, if you have not already done so, to ask your doctor or a friend using a private aid to recommend a dispenser. Privately dispensed aids are sold through four main channels.

First, there is the *specialist hearing aid centre* staffed full time and in many cases fully equipped.

Second, some *dispensers are located in other retail premises* such as chemists or opticians. The dispenser will then be available by appointment as he visits the outlet weekly on prescribed days.

Third, there are *travelling exhibitions* usually held in local hotels. The title 'exhibition' is generally a misnomer since the supply and dispensation of hearing aids is a service which cannot be 'exhibited'. The Hearing Aid Council has laid down that:

> '*Dispensers and employers taking part in any exhibition or public demonstration of hearing aids away from their own permanent places of business (other than trade or medical exhibitions at which aids are not on sale or offered to the public) shall ensure that adequate provision for subsequent refitting and service is available. The full name and registered Head Office address must be prominently displayed.*'

Lastly, the hearing aid dispenser may visit you *at your home* usually in response to a newspaper advertisement. Home visits are subject to stringent Hearing Aid Council provisions. Before a home visit may be made you must have requested or agreed to the visit subject to the following:

- The visit must take place on a particular day.
- Written notice must, whenever practicable, be sent to you confirming the agreed day, date, approximate time and the name of the dispenser. If this notice is not sent the dispenser must record why it was not practicable to do so.
- Where the dispenser requests permission to visit you at home, the written notice must be accompanied by a first-class pre-paid reply card giving you the opportunity to decline or alter the appointment. The visit

must be at least ten calendar days after the despatch of the notice by first-class post.

o The dispenser may not charge for a home visit or test unless you have agreed to the charge before the day of the visit. The written notice mentioned above must contain details of the charge.

The Hearing Aid Council has specified that irrespective of the location a dispenser shall have the following equipment available for use at every consultation.

o A pure tone audiometer which contains facilities for both air and bone conduction audiometry with masking which is calibrated to prescribed British, European and International standards.

o An otoscope and specula with facilities for cleaning them.

o Suitable aural impression material and associated equipment.

o When required the dispenser must also be able to arrange speech audiometry.

Private hearing aids are not cheap. However, the prescription of the most appropriate aid can also significantly increase your enjoyment of enhanced hearing. Before purchasing an aid you should therefore give consideration to the following:

o Try to locate a dispenser within reasonable distance of your home to save unnecessary expense and inconvenience should your aid require attention.

o Tell the dispenser the type of aid you would prefer, for example, behind-the-ear, in-the-ear, spectacle, and so forth, and ask whether such an aid is appropriate to your hearing loss and obtainable at the price you wish to pay.

o Let the dispenser know about the possible environments in which the aid is likely to be worn, for example, at home, in a noisy factory.

o A good dispenser will normally test your ability to discriminate speech sounds as well as pure tones.

o Although modern commercial hearing aids are customized to provide hearing enhancement at those frequencies where according to your audiogram you have a loss, do not expect the hearing aid dispenser to prescribe with the same precision as an optician.

o If, on the first visit to a private dispenser, you decide to purchase one or possibly two aids (if it is considered that you would benefit from binaural fitting), you will be asked to make a deposit against the total price. This deposit may be refunded wholly or in part if you decide not to purchase. On delivery, you will be required to pay the balance of the price. In the unlikely event of the instrument(s) proving to be unsuitable, and being returned in new condition within an agreed number of days from the date of supply, the dispenser will, under the terms of a stated *Returns Privilege* refund either the whole or part of the purchase price. While an instrument is in your possession, treat it carefully, test it fairly and, if you decide not to complete the purchase, return it promptly.

- Only *YOU* can decide which aid is most satisfying from the standpoints of comfort, speech intelligibility and tonal quality.

The Hearing Aid Council states that before providing or effecting the provision or a hearing aid or aids and before you enter into a commitment to purchase if this should be later, the dispenser must provide you with written information regarding:

- The make and model of the aid/aids to be supplied.
- The cash price including VAT for the hearing aid and details of any additional charges and any alternative terms as required by law if credit terms or rental are offered.
- The precise terms of the Return Privilege.
- The terms and conditions, if any, under which you may cancel the order and the terms and details of any refund which may be available.
- The name, address and telephone number of the dispenser and the firm, if different:

  (1) supplying the hearing aid

  (2) whom you should contact to exercise any rights in relation to the trial period, cancellation or refund

  (3) whom you should contact to obtain batteries, repairs or service.

- The terms of any guarantee.
- An undertaking to arrange a further personal consultation with you at no charge at the place of the original consultation or wherever you agree within six weeks of the supply of the hearing aid/aids, to assess your progress and offer any assistance that may be required.
- A statement that one of the above affects your statutory rights.

A copy of the Supply Form issued in conformity with the Hearing Aid Council Code of Practice is shown in *Appendix 2*.

Hearing Aid Fitting

Fitting a hearing aid, whether an NHS or private instrument, is a mixture of science and art. In determining what aid is most suitable for your loss, NHS audiology technicians or private hearing aid dispensers should consider all the medical, audiological and psychological evidence available.

Medical Evidence relates to the type and cause of the hearing impairment, ie conductive, sensorineural, mixed loss and its long-term prognosis.

Audiological Evidence is obtained from pure tone and speech testing and should include:

- Your *hearing threshold* by both air and bone conduction in respect of each ear. This will also provide information on the degree of hearing loss at each frequency tested and the configuration of your loss.
- Your *speech discrimination scores* for each ear.
- Your *MCL* or *most comfortable loudness level.*
- Your *degree of recruitment.*

Psychological Evidence relates to such matters as:

- Your personal motivation for wishing to obtain an aid
- Pressure exerted by relatives, friends, work colleagues and professionals on you to obtain help
- Your expectations in relation to what the aid will achieve.

Other relevant factors can include your age, manual dexterity and the environments in which the aid will be worn.

Of the above factors one of the most important is speech discrimination. Although Raymond Carhart, an American audiologist, advocated as long ago as 1946 that the selection of the most suitable aid should be based on speech discrimination rather than the direct matching of electroacoustic/psychoacoustic data, there is evidence that because of the time involved, word discrimination and speech-in-the-noise testing is not always used in the prescription of hearing aids.

On the basis of the above data, the task of the hearing aid technician or dispenser is to select an instrument that will enable you to obtain the maximum benefit from your residual hearing. Maryanne Tate[1] has summarized the basic priorities for the initial prescription of hearing aid characteristics as:

---

1   Tate, M. (1994) *Principles of Hearing Aid Audiology.* London: Chapman and Hall, p. 171.

(1) The correct amount of gain, which is usually approximately equal to half the hearing loss by air condition.

(2) The maximum output which is not greater than the genuine uncomfortable loudness level.

(3) A frequency response that relates to the slope of the audiogram, without over-amplifying the low frequencies.

Binaural or Monaural Fitting

The advantages of binaural hearing aids have been mentioned in Chapter 2. In addition to such obvious advantages of binaural amplification as localization, ability to listen to conversation from both sides and improved sound quality, the supra-threshold summation effect referred to earlier enables equal loudness to be obtained at an intensity level of 6 dB less when two aids are used rather than one. This improves speech discrimination and provides more comfortable hearing in noise.

While binaural amplification is beneficial in most cases of bilateral loss, user objections or audiological factors may in some cases favour fitting only one aid.

User objections are usually on the grounds of:

- The subjective sense of restriction or confinement when both ears are occluded by an aid.

- The psychological feeling of being doubly handicapped when wearing two aids. The illogicality of this objection is that glasses are preferable to a monocle for the correction of a visual impairment. Is it not equally sensible to aid both ears rather than one?

- The high financial outlay on purchasing two aids rather than one. You have to decide whether the enhanced quality of life consequent on binaural amplification is worth the additional outlay.

Audiological factors may also indicate that in your case one aid is preferable. Circumstances in which such circumstances may arise are:

- Where your speech discrimination scores for each ear are widely dissimilar so that feeding amplified sound into the ear with most distortion causes deterioration in the signal transmitted along the acoustic pathway from the better ear.

- Where your *dynamic range* is significantly restricted in one ear. (The dynamic range is found by subtracting your threshold of hearing from your threshold of discomfort.) Such a restricted dynamic range will result in a low tolerance level for amplification.

Where one ear is *dead* and therefore cannot be assisted by an aid. (Here a CROS fitting may be appropriate.)

  o Where you have problems in operating the aid's controls due to limited manual dexterity on one side.

Where there is a possibility of fitting either ear but for some reason only monaural amplification is feasible, the technician or dispenser has to decide which ear to fit.

The general rule is that you should wear your aid in the better ear since normally this will be the one with the best speech discrimination and wider dynamic range.

This is by no means a universal rule. It will probably be advantageous to wear your aid in the *worst* ear if your hearing loss in both ears is only mild or both ears show hearing levels for speech between 30 and 55 dB. In any event the dispenser should take into account your preference and other relevant factors. If, for example, you do a considerable amount of driving, it may be better to wear the aid in the nearest to the centre of the car, thus reducing interference through traffic noise. It might even be that you prefer to wear the aid in the ear nearest your living room door when seated in your favourite chair.

Learning to Use Your Aid

Whether you require an NHS aid or buy a private aid, you must not expect to gain the maximum benefit immediately. Adjustment to a hearing aid is affected by many variables. Your age and personality, the cause and duration of your hearing loss and the environment in which the aid is used all influence the time necessary to adapt to it. Perseverance, common sense and some understanding of the aid itself are essential. A booklet of general guidance is issued with every NHS aid. Some similar publication is usually given to the purchaser of a privately dispensed aid. The following advice is intended to reinforce or supplement that given in such guides.

  o *Recognize the limitations of your aid.* Basically, a hearing aid is an amplifying device. While modern aids are very efficient, not even the best aid can wholly provide the clear discrimination, selectivity and location of sound that is obtained with normal hearing.

  o *Recognize your own limitations.* Difficulties in adjustment may be due to yourself rather than to the aid. If your hearing loss is of long duration you may have become so conditioned to living in a quiet world that at first you resent rather than welcome the noise in your environment that becomes audible with your aid. Older people may take longer to adjust than younger ones. Presbyacusis and other sensorineural conditions may be accompanied by recruitment so that the margin between your speech Reception Threshold and the overloading of your cochlea is small. Fatigue, nerves and even minor illnesses such as a cold may adversely affect your reception.

o *Become familiar with the aid's operation and controls.* Be sure that you know:

   (1) How to insert and remove the hearing aid(s).

   (2) What battery(ies) to use and how to insert or remove it/them.

   (3) How to use the volume control.

   (4) Operation of on–off switch.

   (5) Use of telecoil or telephone.

   (6) How to clean the aid.

o *Use the aid at first in your home environment.* Concentrate on listening to and identifying normal household sounds such as the electric cleaner, the tinkling of cups and running water.

o *Don't be discouraged by the interference of background noises.* Your aid amplifies noise as well as speech. People with normal hearing are also aware of background noise but have learned to push it out of their conscious awareness. As you learn to discriminate between noise and speech and to identify background sounds you will also adjust to extraneous sound.

o *Gradually increase the number of situations in which you use your aid.* After you have learned to adjust to your own background noise and conversing with several persons at once, extend the use of your aid to the supermarket, church and other public places.

o *Use the controls intelligently.* If you have difficulty in quiet surroundings you should turn up the volume. Conversely, if you are in noisy surroundings or outside on a windy day it is sensible to turn the volume down. Make use of the telephone coil when applicable.

o *Only wear the aid as long as it is comfortable to do so.* At first you may find the use of an aid fatiguing. If you feel tired after using the aid for an hour or two, take it off. As you become more accustomed to the instrument you may eventually be able to use it all day without being aware that you are doing so.

o *Let your dispenser know of any problems.* Most dispensers will ask to see you after you have used the aid for about three weeks. This is the time to tell the dispenser whether the aid appears *tinny*, *harsh* or *too loud*. The dispenser will be able to make adjustment to the tone and automatic volume controls or modify the ear mould. You should never attempt to make such adjustments yourself.

Maintaining the Aid

The routine attention you can give to your aid is limited to the batteries, ear mould, cord (on body-worn aids) and the short plastic tube feeding into the channel of the ear mould on most behind-the-ear instruments. As said earlier, the term *plumbing* is sometimes used to refer to the tubing and ear mould. Advice on the maintenance of the aid will be given in the instruction book supplied when the instrument is issued or purchased and should be carefully read. In particular you should pay attention to the following:

- See that batteries used are new, of the type specified for your aid and correctly inserted.

- Remove batteries immediately they are spent or if you do not intend to use the aid for any length of time.

- Return used batteries to your hearing centre or dispenser if requested to do so.

- Never leave batteries where small children or pets can reach them. If, inadvertently, they are swallowed, call a doctor immediately.

- Clean the ear mould regularly by washing it in warm soapy water, removing any wax from the channel with a pipe cleaner. The mould should, of course, first be detached from the earphone on a body-worn aid or the plastic tube on a behind-the-ear instrument.

- In-the-ear aids must not be washed. Wipe them periodically with a dry tissue and see that the sound outlet and vent where appropriate is free from wax. Wax can be removed by a special wax removal tool or cleaning brush, or a special solvent, both normally available from your dispenser.

- Use an air blower or *puffer* to remove condensation from the plastic tubing.

- The plastic tube may eventually become stiff and even break, although it is easy to replace.

Looking after a hearing aid is, after all, largely a matter of common sense. Hearing aids are delicate instruments and should not be dropped, exposed to temperature extremes or immersed in water. They should be removed in potentially damaging situations such as washing, shaving or before using a hairspray.

You might also give consideration to two further suggestions.

○ Look ahead. Keep an emergency pack comprising a supply of batteries, a length of appropriately sized plastic tubing and, if you use a body-worn aid, a spare cord. You will then not be inconvenienced if you are unable to get replacement items immediately.

○ Hearing aids are becoming increasingly small and, in any event, are valuable instruments. It is, therefore, advisable to insure them against loss or theft. premiums re not high and should be discussed with your insurance company or broker. In any event, hearing aids can be added to a good household insurance policy.

Apart from the simple maintenance hints given above, the warning that you should never attempt to interfere with the interior of the aid is worth reiterating. It is useful, however, to be able to identify possible faults and the following checklist may be helpful.

What if a Hearing Aid is no Use?

If, due to profound deafness, little or no benefit is derived from a conventional hearing aid, you may be helped by a vibro-tactile aid or a cochlea implant.

A vibro-tactile aid transmits information about acoustic stimuli especially speech through the skin. A typical vibro tactile aid comprises a vibrating pad usually worn on a wrist strap to resemble a watch. As shown by Figure 6.7, the device comprises a microphone and a processing unit.

The microphone picks up an acoustic signal and transduces it into an electric signal. The unit processes the signal and sends it to the tactile transducer(s) which deliver vibratory or electrical patterns to the skin. With practice, users of vibro tactile aids can learn to recognize varying vibratory patterns derived from different acoustic stimuli. The aspects of acoustic signals most easily detected are the presence or absence of sound, sound duration, sound patterns and pitch information. Tactile aids are particularly useful as an adjunct to lip reading since it is considered that only about 30 per cent of speech can be lipread. Wearers of tactile aids report that they feel less isolated because of their enhanced awareness of environmental sound. Other benefits include avoiding the embarrassment of inadvertently interrupting conversation, recognition of bird song, recognition of cars approaching from behind in a country lane.

Although advantageous, vibro tactile aids can only provide quite limited help. This is because the transmission of acoustic information via the skin is inevitably less sensitive than through the auditory system.

Many people who might benefit from a vibro tactile aid may also be considered for a cochlea implant. Cochlea implants are discussed in Chapter 7.

Some Common Hearing Aid Problems

Problem	Item to check	Possible cause	Suggested action
No sound	1 earmould	channel blocked with wax	clean earmould
	2 batteries	battery spent	replace with new battery
		battery wrongly inserted	insert correctly
		battery contacts dirty	return to hearing aid centre or dispenser for cleaning
	3 plastic tube	condensation in the tube	blow through the tube (first remove the ear mould if appropriate) or use a **puffer**. NEVER blow into the aid itself
	4 cord (on body-worn aids)	cord broken or damaged	replace cord
Low output from aid	battery	battery almost spent	replace battery
	volume control	wrong setting	adjust control
	T switch	not returned to the M position after use	return to M position
Crackling	cord or cord plug on body-worn aids	damaged cord	replace cord
	battery	poor contact)	return to hearing centre or dispenser for cleaning
	volume control	dirty volume control)	
Squealing or whistling (feedback) or volume needed to be turned down below required level to obviate whistling	insertion	aid wrongly inserted ear itself blocked with wax	insert aid correctly see doctor
	earmould or vent	earmould insufficiently tight or vent too large	return to centre or dispenser for rectification

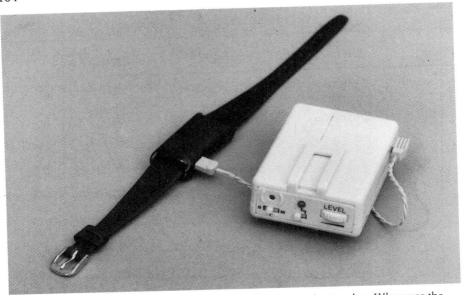

Wear the TAM like a watch with the control box in a convenient pocket. Whenever the TAM picks up a sound above the level set by you the wrist band will vibrate.

Figure 6.7

Conversation Aids

These are electronic or non-electronic devices used to facilitate conversation between two people, one of whom is hard of hearing and, for some reason, unable to use a conventional hearing instrument. Conversational aids will, for example, be useful in hospitals, when talking to elderly people and for medical consultants. Electronic aids comprise a small hand held unit with a built in microphone, an amplifier and a headphone or headphones.

Non-electrical aids are old-fashioned ear trumpets and listening tubes in which the speaker speaks into the trumpet, horn or tube and the listener places an earpiece to the ear.

Ear trumpets can be provided under the NHS after referral by your GP. Electronic devices are much cheaper than hearing aids. A useful leaflet, *Conversation Aids*, giving details of suppliers and prices is obtainable from the RNID.

Environmental Aids

Many hearing-impaired people find that a hearing aid enables them to cope satisfactorily with all the auditory requirements of daily life. there are others, however, who due to the severity of their hearing loss, need additional help from what are termed environmental aids or assistive hearing devices.

A quotation from a survey made in 1972 of people with hearing difficulties living in Balby, Leicestershire, called attention to the way in which many such people could be helped by relatively simple aids. Twenty years later this quotation has lost none of its relevance.

'Many of the housewives described how they missed hearing door bells, thus annoying tradespeople and missing friends. On the occasion when a caller was expected, they described how they would stay in the front rooms of the house in order to see him; much anxiety might have been saved by a flashing light door bell. One mother used to sit on the stairs in the hall when she was alone and her husband on night shift so she could hear her children if they cried. A major source of tension in many households centred around television viewing. For some households television viewing is one of the main interests outside working hours, but at loud volume can disturb neighbours, children in bed and irritate beyond measure normally hearing people in the family. The alternative means that the heard of hearing person is excluded. Once again a gadget could have saved many hours of tension.'

Such *gadgets* or *assistive listening devices* include:

- loud doorbells
- visual doorbell systems
- flashing or vibrating bedside alarms (eg clocks, baby alarms)
- fire alarms (eg visual or vibrating)
- smoke detectors (eg with a vibrating pad)
- listening devices for television, including microphone or plug-in listening aids, amplified headphones, loop systems and infra-red systems
- televisions or television adaptors to enable subtitle reception
- telephone aids including
- amplifiers or inductive couplers for use with personal hearing aids
- keyboard and visual display communication systems
- loud telephone bells and vibrating or visual signals.

It would be impracticable to attempt a detailed description of the above aids. Fortunately it is not necessary to do since there are two publications that every person who may benefit from their use can obtain free. The first is *Solutions – a guide to products for deaf and hard of hearing people* published by the RNID subsidiary, Sound Advantage. The second is The BT *Guide for People who are disabled or elderly.* If you browse through these guides you are almost certain to find a device which will meet your particular need. It is also worth discussing any environmental problem with a hearing therapist or hearing aid dispenser. One useful feature of the current (1994) BT Guide is a list of Disabled Living Centres. These centres, located in most major cities, specialize in demonstrating equipment for disabled people. Displays of environmental aids for hearing-impaired people are often provided in hospital audiology or occupational therapy departments and by specialized centres for deaf or hard of hearing people.

Obtaining Environmental Aids

Environmental aids can be purchased either directly from the manufacturers or suppliers as with BT equipment or through intermediaries such as Sound Advantage or a hearing aid dispenser.

Help in obtaining environmental aids for daily living or employment may also be obtainable through Social Services Departments or Job Centres.

Help for Daily Living

The Chronically Sick and Disabled Persons Act 1970 (S2(1)) does not mention daily living equipment in general except by reference to *additional facilities designed to secure ... greater safety, comfort or convenience*. The Act does, however, make specific reference to telephones (aids to use the telephone), television and radio.

If, therefore, you have a severe to profound hearing loss and the provision of appropriate daily living equipment would reduce your dependence on others or greatly improve your quality of life, it is possible that some help with the provision of environmental aids might be given.

You should first apply to your local Social Services Department stating what help you need and why. A letter of support from your general practitioner, hearing therapist or social worker is helpful.

You will then be assessed for help either in your own home or elsewhere such as a hearing aid centre or perhaps the local voluntary society for deaf people where the society has an agency agreement to provide services for deaf and hard-of-hearing people on behalf of a local authority.

Social Services Departments differ in their criteria for the provision of daily living equipment. They may, for example, distinguish between what is *necessary* and what is *desirable* and only aid the former. They may also lay down conditions. The Social Services Department may agree to provide a flashing telephone or door bell alerting you to callers conditional on your accepting liability for the installation of the telephone line, appropriate sockets and the handset. Because arrangements differ widely between Social Services Departments, only an outline of what can be done is practicable.

Equipment for Employment

Many Social Services Departments lay down that daily living equipment must not be used for employment or business purposes. If, due to your hearing impairment you need special equipment to obtain or retain a job or work on your own account, help may be available under the Department of Employment's Access to Work Scheme. Under this Scheme each applicant may receive assistance to the value of £21,000 over five years although most people will require much less. Equipment that may typically be provided to people with hearing impairments includes amplifiers, loud speaking telephone aids, communicators, communicating terminals, computers and adaptations to switchboards.

Applications for help under the Access to Work Scheme should be made by your employer or yourself to the Disability Employment Adviser at your Job Centre who will arrange for a Placing, Assessment and Counselling Team (PACT) to decide if and what equipment or adaptations are required.

7
Cochlear Implants

Cochlea implantation is a dramatic breakthrough in the auditory rehabilitation of profoundly hearing-impaired people for whom hearing aids provide little or no benefit. This section attempts to provide some information about what cochlea implants are, how potential candidates are assessed, what is involved and the risks and benefits of this procedure.

What is a Cochlear Implant?

Essentially, a cochlear implant is an alternative form of hearing instrument applicable to some people who, because of bilateral sensorineural loss due to cochlear failure, are unable to benefit from even the most powerful conventional hearing aid.

Cochlear failure arises from damage to the tiny hair cells which are each connected to a fibre of the auditory nerve (viii nerve). Due to this damage the hair cells are unable to transmit sound for processing by the brain. Although the hair cells are damaged, however, some auditory fibres and the auditory nerve are often still functional. In such cases it is possible to create a sensation of sound by direct electrical stimulation of the auditory nerve. A cochlear implant, therefore, is a device designed to stimulate the hearing nerve with electrical impulses. In other words it is an acoustic transducer that changes sound into electrical energy which can be received and conducted by the auditory nerve. The electrical signals are then interpreted by the brain as sound.

The Parts of a Cochlear Implant System

The components of a cochlear implant system are shown in Figure 7.1 and can be divided into internal and external parts.

(A) The Cochlear Implant

The *internal* part (A) is the cochlear implant itself, which the surgeon 'implants' in the bone behind one ear. The implant has a magnet, a receiver/decoder with a small 'tail' which contains the electrode bands extending into the inner ear. (An electrode is one of the terminals, positive or negative of an electric current.) Some

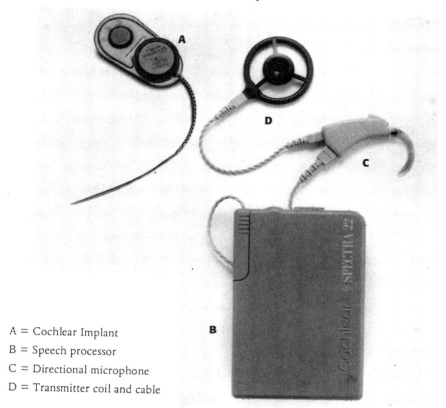

A = Cochlear Implant
B = Speech processor
C = Directional microphone
D = Transmitter coil and cable

Figure 7.1 Nucleus cochlear implant system

implants have only one electrode band on the tail and are termed 'single-channel'. Implants with up to 22 electrode bands are described as 'multi-channel'. another factor is the actual location of the 'tail' in the inner ear. Normally with single-channel implants the 'tail' is placed at the entrance to the cochlea on the round window and is termed 'extra-cochlea'. With multi-channel implants, the 'tail' is inserted quite deeply into the cochlea and is, therefore, described as 'intra-cochlea'.

The current experience is that multi-channel intra-cochlea implants provide superior speech recognition in comparison with single channel stimulation.

The external parts of the system comprise (B) the speech processor; (C) the directional microphone and (D) the transmitter coil and cable.

(B) The Speech Processor

With most systems the speech processor resembles a body-worn hearing aid or small transistor radio, although there are behind-the-ear processors. As implied by its name, the speech processor's function is to select and code the sounds most useful for understanding speech and can be programmed individually to provide the user with the best possibilities for hearing with the implant. The speech processor also houses the battery or batteries and has controls enabling the user to adjust for sensitivity and volume.

(C) The directional microphone
   and

(D) Transmitter, Coil and Cable
   The microphone fits behind the ear and picks up sound. A thin cord carries the signal from the microphone to the speech processor and also the processed signal back to the transmitter which codes the signal for radio transmission through the skin to the implanted receiver. The receiver decodes the signal and sends the pattern of impulses to the electrode in the cochlea where the electrode bands produce small electrical impulses according to the pattern decoded by the receiver. These impulses stimulate the auditory nerve which generates nerve impulses. These nerve impulses, when received by the brain, are interpreted as acoustic events so that the implant user experiences a hearing sensation.

   With so called *transcutaneous* implants such as the Nucleus 22 multi-channel device shown the transmitter is held firmly in place over the internal receiver by a pair of magnets, one located under the skin and the second in the centre of the external transmitter.

   The whole process described above in relation to a Nucleus 22 multi-channel transcutaneous cochlea implant is shown diagrammatically in Figure 7.2.

Assessment of Suitability for a Cochlear Implant

   If you consider that you might benefit from a cochlear implant, the first step is to ask your general practitioner to refer you to one of the UK Cochlear Implant Centres.

   Currently (1995) there are centres located in Birmingham, Bradford, Cambridge, London (University College/Middlesex Hospital), Manchester, Middlesborough, Nottingham, Sheffield, Edinburgh, Kilmarnock, Bridgend, Badelwyddan (Rhyl) and Belfast. Nottingham is the only paediatric centre in the UK specializing in implants for children aged five years and under. Although an expensive procedure, costing between £20,000 and £35,000, cochlea implantation is undertaken at the above hospitals under the NHS.

   The Implant Centre may then send you a questionnaire for completion to determine whether you satisfy the preliminary criteria for further consideration

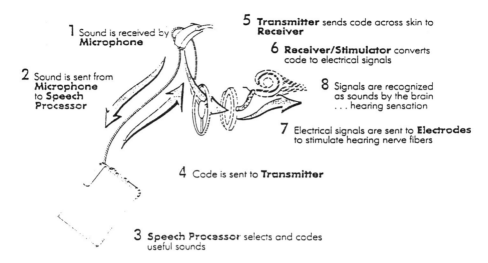

1 Sound is received by **Microphone**

2 Sound is sent from **Microphone** to **Speech Processor**

3 **Speech Processor** selects and codes useful sounds

4 Code is sent to **Transmitter**

5 **Transmitter** sends code across skin to **Receiver**

6 **Receiver/Stimulator** converts code to electrical signals

7 Electrical signals are sent to **Electrodes** to stimulate hearing nerve fibers

8 Signals are recognized as sounds by the brain . . . hearing sensation

Figure 7.2 How a cochlea implant system produces hearing sensation, step by step.
(Courtesy of Cochlea Pty Ltd)

as an implant candidate, together with an information pack explaining what an implant involves. In general, you will not be considered for an implant unless:

- you have a profound sensorineural hearing loss in both ears
- you derive no benefit from the most powerful hearing aids
- you possess the linguistic skills necessary to participate in the post-operative programme of rehabilitation and evaluation. Adults born with a profound sensorineural hearing loss are, therefore, not generally suitable for implantation.

Age is, however, no barrier to selection. The information pack issued by the Midlands Cochlear Implant and Rehabilitation Programme at Queen Elizabeth Hospital, Birmingham, refers to 'Jack' then aged 86, who became totally deaf at the age of 78. 'Jack' states:

> 'I always use my implant for the whole day and for me it has made a wonderful change to my life, as now I can go out on my own and talk with people . . .
>
> To any deaf person that has the chance for this wonder I say "GO FOR IT".'

On the basis of your answers to the questionnaire, the Implant Centre team will decide whether to invite you to undergo further tests. There are two reasons why these tests are time consuming.

First, as stated above, cochlea implantation is done on a team basis. You will be assessed by every member of the team. In addition to the consultant Otologist who undertakes the surgery and is responsible for making the final decision regarding your suitability for fitting, the team comprises:

- The **audiological scientist** – undertakes the assessment of your pre- and post-operative hearing and the actual 'tuning' of the implant.
- The **speech therapist** – concerned with the assessment and conservation of your speech and post-operative adjustment to hearing.
- The **hearing therapist** – responsible for providing counselling and support to you and your family on how to use the implant and what other assistance is needed and where and how it can be obtained.
- The **clinical psychologist** – determines whether you have the motivation, personality and intelligence to cope adequately with the pre- and post-operative procedures involved.

Second, as indicated by the different disciplines represented in the implant team, assessment of suitability requires the consideration of a wide range of audiological, medical/otological and psychological criteria.

- **Audiological assessment** includes standard pure tone and other hearing tests, hearing aid fitting and tests of speech understanding with and without lip-reading. These tests aim to ascertain whether greater benefit can be expected from a cochlea implant. They also provide a baseline for comparison with your performance after the implant is fitted.
- **Medical/otological assessment** involves tests of general health, general anaesthesia, absence of chronic active ear disease, tests of balance and the state of the cochlea itself as indicated by a Computed Tomography (CT) scan. A CT scan is a process of X-raying a patient to show slices through the body which allow a three-dimensional understanding. A CT scan of the skull can enable the otologist to check that your cochlea is clear of any bony growth or scar tissue so that an electrode can be inserted.
- **Psychological testing**, as stated earlier, is carried out to ensure that you are well motivated, have realistic expectations of the outcome and a readiness to participate in post-operative auditory and speech training.

If invited to undergo such assessment, you should certainly accept. You have nothing to lose and much to gain. Before attending, you should read as much as possible about cochlea implants. A very useful booklet, *An Introduction to Cochlea Implants*, is available from the National Association of Deafened People. It is also useful to meet an actual implant user.

Make a list of queries you wish to raise at the assessment and do not be afraid to ask. Even if you are considered unsuitable for an implant, the Centre will suggest other ways in which you may possibly be helped. If, however, you are deemed suitable for and accept the offer of an implant, the next stages are those of the actual operation and the post-operative rehabilitation.

The Operation

The waiting time between assessment and admission to hospital varies according to the Centre from three to four months to over a year. Most centres have a policy that patients will not be implanted earlier than six months after the onset of profound bilateral hearing loss.

The stay in hospital varies between two and seven days after the operation. The aim of the operation is to implant the receiver behind the ear and, in the case of an intra-cochlea device, insert the electrode through the Scala Tympani into the cochlea for a distance of about 25 mm, which is about one-and-a-half turns of the coil.

Prior to the operation, the hair behind the selected ear is shaved off to eliminate infection. This soon grows again. The operation itself is performed under general anaesthesia and takes between two and four hours. To reach the cochlea the surgeon has to drill through the mastoid bone. Before the electrode can be inserted in the cochlea, a small hole has to be made in the inner ear using a fine drill of 1–2 mm diameter. In addition, a recess has to be made in the bone of the skull just behind the mastoid to accommodate the receiver. The initial incision behind the ear is quite large, but heals rapidly and the stitches are removed after a week to ten days. Normally, patients are up and about within two days of the operation. Most people are completely back to normal after two weeks.

The risks, apart from those attendant on any operation involving general anaesthesia, include disturbance or damage to the facial nerve, disturbance of taste or balance, infection round the implant and tinnitus changes. Skilled surgery combined with scrupulous attention to asepsis (prevention of infection) during the operation and the use of antibiotics make such risks minimal. It should be recognized, however, that intra-cochlea implantation will, very likely, destroy any residual natural nearing in the operated ear. Since implantation is a comparatively recent development, the long term effects are not known.

The 'Switch On'

The external parts of an implant – the speech processor, directional microphone and the transmitter coil and cable – are received by the patient at the 'switch-on' which takes place some four to six weeks after the operation when the wound has completely healed. During this interval, the operated ear will be kept under surveillance by the otologist.

At 'switch-on' the audiological scientist, using a specially developed computer program and assisted by the patient, seeks to find the most appropriate speech processor settings for the implantee. This involves a complex process of ascertaining hearing thresholds at given frequencies and increasing the intensities until a volume is reached which is perceived as loud but not uncomfortable. When these events have been established, each of the electrodes can be 'fine-tuned' one by one for a particular pitch and loudness to provide the speech signals suitable for the implantee (see Figure 7.3). Further adjustments will take place over the next few months.

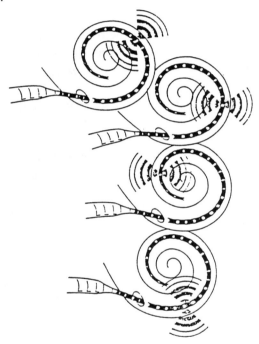

Figure 7.3. 22 electrodes fine-tuned 'one-by-one'. (Courtesy Nuclear Pty. Ltd)

At the switch-on the patient is also instructed in the use of the external parts of the system, including the positioning of the transmitter, the wearing of the speech processor, how to change the batteries and the use of the speech processor controls.

'Switch-on' will be followed by an auditory training programme conducted by the hearing and speech therapists. In this programme the patient learns to identify individual sounds, to discriminate noises from speech and gradually to recognize such aspects of speech as vowels, consonants, syllables, words and sentences. Progress will usually be monitored by speech tests which, by comparing pre-operative performance with results over a period of time, indicate what help the user is obtaining from the implant.

Cochlear Implant Pros and Cons

There are currently no standardized procedures by which the benefit likely to be obtained from a cochlear implant by a given individual can be accurately predicted. This is understandable when it is recognized that, while all potential implantees have the common characteristic of profound hearing loss, they vary widely n respect of age, cause and duration of hearing loss and the number of functioning nerve fibres left in the inner ear. There are also a number of different implant devices and approaches to evaluating the results. In general, it has been found that:

o   Adults who have been recently deafened are more likely to be 'stars' than those who have been deafened for many years.

o   Those who have been deafened after acquiring speech and language derive greater benefit from implants than persons with pre-lingual deafness.

In evaluating implants, it is also necessary to know their limitations and disadvantages:

o   Implants are not 'bionic ears'.

o   They do not provide normal hearing – at first they will be robotic and 'tinny'.

o   An implant does not enable the user to discern the direction from which a sound comes.

o   Implants cannot help all people with a profound hearing loss.

o   Some activities that might damage or displace the implant should be avoided. When swimming, the external parts of the implant must be removed.

o   Some medical procedures such as Resonance Imaging (MRI) must not be used in the vicinity of the implant or diathermy applied over the receiver or electrode lead of the implant.

o   Although the majority of implant users report a diminution of tinnitus, in a few cases tinnitus is enhanced.

- The benefits of an implant accrue over time and users need to make consistent use of their hearing and not be discouraged if early results are not up to expectations.
- Like all mechanical devices, an implant may fail and, long term, the speech processor and other external parts may need to be replaced as they wear out; they are, however, designed to last for many years.

Allowing for the variability of results and the limitations and disadvantages, there is little doubt that the overwhelming majority of users report an enhanced quality of life. The 154 recipients of a Nucleus multi-channel implant, who responded to a survey, identified the following benefits:

- 90% felt they were better able to communicate.
- 82% had increased confidence.
- 62% reported more social opportunities.
- 33% indicated improved job performance.
- 28% felt they had additional job opportunities.

More specifically, the benefits mentioned by implantees include:

- Improved ability to recognize speech when hearing through the implant is combined with lip-reading.
- Some users are able to understand a significant amount of speech and carry on one-to-one conversations when hearing through the implant alone.
- A survey indicated that 51% of 146 Nucleus implant receivers reported that through the implant they were able to understand speech well enough to engage in a two way telephone conversation with a familiar speaker.
- Increased recognition of environmental sounds helping to reduce the depression resulting from the loss of background noise reported in Chapter 5, providing greater safety and enhanced aesthetic pleasure, for example, listening to bird sounds.
- Ability to monitor the volume and quality of the implant user's voice.

While recognizing that an implant will benefit some users more than others, the experience of Alison Heath, currently Hon. Secretary of the National Association of Deafened People, will be a source of interest and encouragement to all concerned with implants in particular and hearing impairment in general:

A World Lost and Regained

The first eight years of my life were spent happily as one of the younger members of a quite a large family in wartime Britain. At the end of the war disaster overtook me – an untreated ear infection led to bacterial meningitis and left me with one completely deaf ear.

It was not until I went to school that the full extent of my hearing loss really hit me. In spite of a front seat in class I had difficulty keeping up. For a time I persevered and also kept up with my piano lessons but it was not to be. I heard 'funny noises' in my head and my hearing became erratic, changing from day to day – I was not coping and deafness was something that the teaching staff at my school did not understand.

My father, himself a hearing aid user, came to my rescue. I was fitted out with a large, clumsy, hearing aid to which I did not initially take. Finally, even with the help of the aid, it became clear that I had no chance of academic success without special support in a normal school. I spent the last four years of my schooling at the Mary Hare Grammar School but I felt something of a misfit. I was essentially a deafened person who felt more at home in the hearing world than the deaf one.

When I reached university my lipreading was still poor because I was trying to use the remains of my erratic hearing. However I was determined not to be outdone and three myself into my studies and university life. I have always had one great love – horses. This hobby proved to be a great icebreaker and it was through active participation in the university horse-manship club that I made many friends and met my future husband.

We married soon after coming down and I tried to find a job. It was a bitter pill to find that I was not at all sought after in the job market but eventually I managed, with the help of the University Appointments Board, to find a post as a trainee librarian. I qualified the hard way by part-time study and was promoted to a professional position as a cataloguer. This was a job that did not make impossible demands on me as a deaf person as I had no contact with the public and I did not need to use the telephone.

Then the family arrived, two daughters and one son and I took a career break for nine years. We were and are a happy family – the children adapted to my deafness. They all speak very clearly and learnt from an early age how to make themselves lipreadable and to attract my attention. My husband has always helped me to remain 'au fait' with all their goings on by relaying things I miss – even all their childish worries that they tended to confide in him if he was there as Mum was rather slow on the uptake.

In 1982 some information about cochlear implants came my way. I was interested and soon found myself undergoing assessment at University

College Hospital. I was given one of the first single channel implants – the 3M Viennese device. It took a while for the benefits to become apparent but the rediscovery of the world of sound was immensely exciting. Hearing the dog bark, the telephone ring, the pips on the radio announcing the news and, above all, the human voice, especially my own, was wonderful. In fact the first thing that people noticed was the change in my voice – it was better modulated and the pitch dropped. Over the years, helped and encouraged by the UCH cochlea implant team, my skill with the implant grew, benefiting not only myself but my family, friends and colleagues at work.

I kept my single channel implant for ten years because my surgeon, the late Mr Graham Fraser, encouraged me to wait for the second generation of implants. Also I had a problem common to many who have been deafened after contracting meningitis. There was bony scar tissue in the cochlea canals near the round window. It is only recently that surgeons have developed techniques to drill out a canal to enable them to thread the electrode array of multichannel implants into the cochlea.

Finally, I was offered a new American multichannel device, the Clarion, at St Thomas' Hospital and my health authority agreed to fund it. A few hours after 'the switch on' I was listening to my husband playing the piano – slowly the sound became richer and more melodious than what I was used to hearing with my single channel device. As I work in central London it was not long before I heard the wail of an ambulance's siren but even that was quite musical compared with the nerve-racking screech that I'd heard before. One major advantage of the Clarion is that I am no longer deafened in social situations by a cacophony of noise. A couple of weeks later I realized that not only were environmental sounds improved but I was also getting more assistance with understanding speech. I was beginning to 'eavesdrop' on normal conversations without people having to slow down for me, I was understanding a few words on the telephone and my two year old grandson suddenly became more intelligible.

I am still in the learning phase with my new implant and my audiologist is adjusting the programme to suite me so I look forward to yet more improvements.

The Future of Cochlea Implants

In 1989 the Council of the British Association of Otolaryngologists stated that, in their view, cochlear implants have passed from the stage of research devices to become an established therapy for the deafened. The procedure is now, as stated earlier in this chapter, available through the NHS at a limited number of regionally located hospitals. Meanwhile, research into the development of cochlear implants is continuing in many countries world-wide. It is certain that within the next decade pure and applied research will lead to fairly rapid improvements both in implant procedures and the devices themselves. Some possible developments identified by Rosen in the NADP booklet referred to earlier, include:

- advances in electrode designs and the optional placement of the electrode into the cochlea

- improvements in methods of getting electrical signals from the speech processor to the electrodes and more 'transparent' interfaces, i.e. systems which do not unduly restrict the kind of signals presented to users

- smaller speech processing boxes and genuine ear level processors for multi-channel devices

- better speech processing, including the 'shapening up' of electrode frequency patterns, control of background noise and different processing schemes, say for speech and music

- fitting procedures that are faster, more reliable and less dependent on the subjective responses of the implantee

- other issues relate to the implanting of persons who are not totally deaf and the use of both implants and hearing aids.

Perhaps the best final comment is that cochlea implants can bring hope the hopeless and, as Alison Heath so elegantly says, 'a lost world regained'.

8

Lipreading, Hearing Tactics and Auditory Training

Lipreading

Almost everyone uses vision to supplement the information received through hearing and other senses. We all watch the face of a speaker when we have difficulty in hearing what is being said: even people with normal hearing may be unconscious lipreaders. But what is lipreading? What are its limitations and advantages? How can lipreading be learned and used in everyday situations? In what ways can we supplement lipreading to make it more reliable?

The Basis of Lipreading

Lipreading is the reception of spoken messages through the medium of vision. An alternative term favoured in the USA and also used in Britain is 'speech-reading'. The advocates of speech-reading hold that the term describes the process more accurately. Lipreading implies that only the lips of the speaker are observed. Speech-reading recognizes that the reception of speech involves watching the jaws, tongue and total expression of a speaker as well as the lips. Accordingly, speech-reading may be defined as 'the art of understanding a speaker's thought by watching the movements of his mouth and facial expression'. Arguably both terms give the erroneous impression that speech can be read from the lips as easily as reading a book or newspaper. While speech-reading may be the more technically correct expression, lipreading is the word that is most popularly understood and is therefore used here.

Basically, lipreading is a skill. Spoken language is composed of identifiable 'speech sounds' or phonemes. Phonemes have distinct variations in air pressure that can be sensed by the ear and can be divided into vowels and consonants. Vowels or 'resonated phonemes' provide the energy input of speech. Consonants or 'articulated sounds' make speech intelligible. Vowel sounds are low pitched while consonants are quieter, especially the S's, F's and Th's. Vowels are low pitched while consonants are high pitched. Most hearing impaired people have a loss which is worse in the higher frequencies – high tone or high pitch – and, while able to hear vowel sounds, have difficulty with consonants. As shown by the example below, vowels themselves can never convey meaning but consonants can make the sentence intelligible even though the vowels are omitted.

Vowels	E	A E	OU	E	A
Consonants	W.	W.LK.D	THR..GH	TH.	P.RK

As shown in the following table in English there are about 45 speech sounds of which 28 and 17 are consonants and vowels respectively.

Some consonants are not difficult to see because of the way in which these are formed by the lips and tongue.

Sounds	Lip/tongue movements	Example
p.b.m.	lips compressed	Pa played in the park. Baa, baa, black sheep. Made many meals.
f.u.	lower lip placed against top teeth	Fight for the faith. Vacant vans vanish.
th	tip of tongue between the teeth	Three thick and three thin things.
w	lips puckered	What wet weather we're having.
sh, ch, j	lip pushed outwards	The shepherd shears the sheep.

Other consonants are more difficult to see.

sz	a 'hiss' sound through almost closed teeth	The singing is superb.
v	tongue is pushed up behind the top gum	Remove the red roses from the room.
l	tongue pushed up behind the top teeth – back of tongue is visible	Little and Large like laughter.
t.d.n.	tongue touches the top gums behind the teeth	take tea with the team today
		Don't dare to go near danger.
k.g.ng	back of the tongue meets the junction of the hard/soft palate with the tip of the tongue behind the bottom teeth	The kind king gave a ring.

Vowel sounds, especially the long vowels also have recognizable lip movements. Thus, to give a few examples, vowel sounds such as 'ah' and 'aw' are made with the mouth wide open. For 'oo' the lips are pushed out; with 'er' the lips are apart and for 'ee' they are elongated as if we are smiling.

The Limitations of Lipreading

Many people think that lipreading is a complete substitute for loss of hearing. Nothing could be further from the truth. Lipreading has a number of limitations.

Speech sounds or words may be unrecognizable for several reasons. While in one second about thirteen articulatory movements are made by the average speaker, the eye of the receiver is capable of consciously recording only eight or nine such movements. Approximately 25 per cent of all the sounds produced are therefore missed by the eye. In fact the number of speech movements missed is greater since not all sounds (e.g. 'ng') are visible in the first place. Two experts, Jeffers and Barley, consider that only four out of fourteen identifiable lipreading movements can be consistently recognized under normal viewing conditions — 'the visibility of the remaining movements varying with the speaker, the rate of speech and the transitional characteristics of the speech pattern'.

In addition, many sounds are 'homopheneous'. This means that sounds or words look alike on the lips of the speaker. No lipreader can distinguish between 'p', 'b' and 'm' since, as stated above, they all involve the same lip movements. The lipreader has therefore to distinguish the appropriate sound or word from the general context of the message. In ordinary circumstances we have to decide whether the speaker means 'where' or 'wear' or 'tire' or 'tyre' from the context. Similarly, a lipreader has to choose between 'Ben', 'men' and 'pen' to complete the sentence 'he had ten thousand ...' Clearly the choice of 'men' is made as the most appropriate of alternatives. Lipreading is thus not merely a matter of watching speech movements but of considerable mental effort in making sense from an incompletely perceived message.

Lipreading has other limitations apart from relying on a considerable element of educated guesswork. The usefulness of lipreading is confined to speech. Lipreading offers no help with music, bird songs or warning signals. It is only of limited value in group conversation and is useless if the speaker is behind or out of the range of the lipreader's vision.

As mentioned earlier, a high proportion of speech sounds are invisible. The normal unit of conversation also tends to be the sentence rather than discrete words. The enquiry 'what time would you like your meal?' is spoken as 'Whattimewouldyoulikeyourmeal?' Unless there is visible pause between each word the lipreader has to cope with a flowing series of movements of varying degrees of visibility.

Environmental factors such as lighting and distance also pose problems for the lipreader. Obviously it is not possible to lipread in the dark. The pupils of a lipreader's eyes are constricted if he has to look into a light source situated behind the speaker. While with normal vision it is possible to lipread at distances of up to 24 feet, it is easier to do so at normal conversational distances: about 5 feet is probably the ideal distance.

Speakers also vary in the ease with which they can be lipread. In general it is harder for a lipreader to comprehend a stranger than someone who is familiar. As indicated, lipreading increases in difficulty with the rapidity of a speaker's delivery. Speakers with expressive faces are easier to lipread than the converse. Speakers who look away, put their hands over their mouths, or smoke cigarettes or pipes while speaking pose problems for lipreaders. Bears and moustaches may also present difficulties.

From the above, certain characteristics of lipreading can be identified.

(1) Even for highly accomplished practitioners lipreading involves a considerable element of educated guesswork.

(2) Lipreading, like reading or the hearing of speech, is not a process which endeavours to identify individual words or articulatory movements. Lipreading is a *total* process, the aim being to comprehend the essential thought that is being communicated. In doing this, the lipreader will be alert to contextual and environmental cues, such as key words, the subject under discussion, the environment in which the message is being received and the gestures and facial expressions of the speaker.

(3) Lipreading requires intense concentration and fatigue may cause the lipreader's attention to wander.

The Advantages of Lipreading

Why should a hearing impaired person attempt to learn a skill which, as shown above, has so many drawbacks even for those who attain high proficiency? The answer is that many people with a severe hearing loss have found lipreading to be a worthwhile accomplishment which has amply repaid the time and effort devoted to learning it.

Lipreading may increase the usefulness of both hearing aids and cochlea implants. The usefulness of lipreading in enhancing the benefits obtained from a hearing aid was demonstrated as long ago as 1943 in a series of experiments at Manchester University. These experiments involved ninety unselected persons aged from seventeen to seventy-two who had an acquired hearing loss. Eighty-seven of the participants had attended classes in lipreading. The purpose of the experiment was to ascertain the benefits of increased comprehension that the group members had obtained from lipreading and hearing aids. The following results were reported:

Conditions of Test	Average Score per cent
Ordinary listening without hearing or lipreading	21
Ordinary listening with lipreading	64
Listening with an electronic aid without lipreading	64
Listening with an electronic aid together with lipreading	90

(Sir Alexander and Lady E C Ewing *Hearing Aids, Lipreading and Clear Speech* 1943)

Later experiments have confirmed the enhanced advantages of combining the use of an aid with lipreading. In particular, lipreading may help to overcome discrimination difficulties when a hearing aid user has problems with distortion and recruitment.

The development of cochlear implants have also enabled lipreaders to benefit by the linking of sound to sight. As one lady observed 'lipreading alone is like talking through a pane of glass but with sound it comes to life. It's like the difference between black and white and colour TV'. A deafened general medical practitioner in an amusing article in *Network* (Spring 1994), the newsletter of the National Association of Deafened People, after detailing some problems encountered with homophones and sibilants when attempting to lipread patients observes, 'Interestingly it is only since I had a cochlea implant that I can distinguish between 'rape' and 'scrape', 'breath' and 'breasts', in that I can now hear the S's, F's and Th's.

Lipreading can also be an important psychological help for a person faced by a sudden and irreversible hearing impairment. Learning lipreading is one of the few immediate positive steps that a person in these circumstances can take towards rehabilitation and may help in reducing depression. Lipreading can also reduce the sense of isolation and increase confidence in social situations. Hearing and users know that they will not be completely helpless should their instrument let them down. When asked to name the greatest benefit she had received from a series of lipreading lessons a lady replied 'I am no longer afraid to go shopping'.

Lipreading is particularly important in cases of sensorineural or mixed sensorineural loss; hearing loss that cannot be treated by surgery or when surgery is not acceptable; where the degree of loss is 70 dB or greater over the speech frequencies; and where the usefulness of a hearing aid is reduced by discrimination problems.

Learning to Lipread

The best way of learning lipreading is to join a class. Local Education Authorities will usually provide tuition at a further education college if sufficient persons can be found to form a lipreading class. Lipreading tuition may also be provided on either a class or individual basis at some hospitals. Social workers with deaf people employed by local authority Social Services Departments may also provide lipreading instruction and practice. There are also some private teachers. Overall, however, there is a shortage of lipreading teachers with the consequence that classes may be difficult to find. If you wish to learn lipreading and cannot locate suitable tuition you should contact the Royal National Institute for Deaf People (RNID) or Hearing Concern (The British Association for the Hard of Hearing, BAHOH). The Association of Teachers of Lipreading to Adults (ATLA) aims to improve the standards of lipreading to adults and can also provide information on day and evening lipreading classes.

Lipreading tuition on an individual basis is generally from forty minutes to an hour for each session. Classes tend to be longer and sessions can be from ninety minutes to two hours in duration. The difference is because greater concentration is required if you are taught on an individual basis than if you are a member of a class. Classes are, however, purposely kept small and may be graded to cater for a whole range of lipreaders from beginners to advanced.

If you join a lipreading class you will probably find that the teacher introduces both analytical and synthetical elements into the lesson. The purpose of the analytical element is to train your eyes to recognize speech sounds on the lips of the speaker. The aim of the synthetical element is to train your mind to grasp the total import of a message even though you have not recognized all the individual words. An important part of the instruction will be designed to improve your ability to lipread at speed and to cope with colloquial language, different faces and varying situations. This instruction need not be dull and by using a variety of approaches and activities such as word games and group question and answer sessions, the good teacher can do much to make learning lively and even pleasurable.

No-one would expect to become an expert pianist on the basis of one weekly session with a music teacher. Daily practice is needed if one is to become a proficient lipreader. You need a small mirror and a good friend. The mirror will enable you to see how speech sounds appear on your own lips. Your teacher will give you exercises to practice at home observing in a mirror the speech movements in a sentence such as 'Pa may we all go too' will give invaluable help in mastering the appropriate vowels. The friend cannot only help you with your exercises but also give additional practice with words, numbers and structured sentences. It is important to tell your friend to speak naturally and refrain from exaggerated 'mouthing'. You can also practice lipreading informally with your family at the breakfast table or by observing other people when standing in the bus queue. A number of video tapes have been made for lipreading practice details of which can be obtained from the RNID or BAHOH. Television can also provide excellent lipreading practice though beginners may find that rapidly changing camera views make speakers difficult to follow. When some proficiency has been attained, television can become much more valuable. The practice sessions should be short but frequent: three-quarter hour sessions are better than one of half an hour, since fatigue is less likely.

It is difficult to generalize about how long it will take you to become a proficient lipreader. Natural talent for lipreading is not necessarily the same as high intelligence but it appears that a special attitude similar to trait combinations which make for success in music, art or mechanical skill can be identified. Fusfield, an American researcher in a study of factors making for lipreading success concluded:

> 'No single factor fully accounts for lipreading efficiency but rather a combination of circumstances – natural aptitude, easy command of the English language, acquaintance with the vagaries present in speech and a large functioning vocabulary.'[1]

Lipreading in Practice

In practice, a lipreader will benefit from the following suggestions. If possible combine lipreading with the use of a hearing aid or implant. Remember, as stated above, that lipreading can substantially increase the effectiveness of hearing devices and that the converse is equally true.

Seek the co-operation of the speaker. Admit to your handicap and avoid bluffing. Do not be afraid to tell the speaker that you need to see his or her face clearly. Mention that actions such as putting the hand over the mouth, turning away while speaking or talking and smoking make it difficult or almost impossible for you to lipread. Ask someone who is talking too rapidly to slow down. Normally, when shopping, the salesperson will ring up the prices of your purchases on the till or give you a printed receipt so there should be no misunderstanding. If your lipreading fails ask the speaker to write the message and carry a small notebook or pad for this purpose. Some advice to speakers on how they can help is given in the next section of this chapter.

---

1   Fusfield (1958) 'Factors in lipreading as determined by the lipreader.' *American Annals of the Deaf.* March, pp.230.

Take it for granted that you will have to give more conscious attention to what is said than is necessary for someone with normal hearing If you find it difficult to grasp the message don't give up and retreat into your private thoughts. In the early days of lipreading withdrawal is all too easy and is fatal to your future progress. School yourself to concentrate closely. Regard the situation as a challenge to your ability and a test of your powers of observation.

Think ahead. Try to position yourself strategically so that the speaker faces the light and is at a distance (about five to six feet) at which you can see the whole of his face without difficulty. Consider beforehand what topics of conversation are likely to arise in a pending situation. When shopping, for example, you will be discussing goods and prices; at the doctor you will be asked to describe your symptoms, and so on. In many everyday situations and especially when you know people well you will almost be able to guess the questions you will be asked and even the words they will use. Remember, however, that your anticipations may not be realized and thus avoid the embarrassment of answering questions that have never been asked.

Be alert for clues provided by the speaker, his speech and the situation. Observe the speaker's mood as reflected on his face. Is he serious or light-hearted? Does he look at you questioningly? Does she make use of gestures such as shaking her head or pointing? Notice the rhythm of his speech, his pauses and where he appears to put the emphasis on his words. Use your eyes for clues that may obviate the need for speech. When shopping look for price tags rather than asking how much an article costs. If you know what subject is being discussed you will deal confidently with homopheneous words. For instance, if you are uncertain whether the speaker said 'bill', 'pill' or 'mill' you can almost without thinking choose the appropriate word from the context. Obviously, if the topic of conversation is the cost of heating and lighting, the right word will probably be 'bill', 'pill' is appropriate when health or contraception are under discussion, while 'mill' is likely if the topic is the economic history of the cotton industry.

Most people experience some tension when lipreading due to the need to concentrate and the possibility of making a mistake. This tension may reduce your lipreading efficiency. The aim should be to cultivate alertness without being tense. The study by Fusfield mentioned in the previous section noted:

'One common denominator was present in all skilled lipreaders. This was a personality make-up that did not shake under initial failure, or was not "floored" when things went wrong lipreading-wise. Thus invariably, if the lipreader did not immediately catch on the reaction was "Beg Pardon?" or "I'm sorry, I didn't get you" – so inviting repetition with greater care.' (Fusfield 1958, p.242)

A basic confidence coupled with a sense of humour that will enable you to laugh at rather than be shattered by your mistakes is a priceless lipreading asset.

Hearing Tactics

There are many 'tactics' that a person can use to improve receptive communication in adverse listening conditions. Lack of awareness of such tactics can contribute to the disability of a hearing impaired person. The following list of hearing tactics is adapted from a questionnaire prepared by Field and Haggard[2] which provides an inventory of tactics which can be widely employed under three headings.

Tactics involving manipulating social interaction

- Ask speaker to talk slowly
- Ask speaker to talk loudly
- Ask speaker to talk clearly
- Ask speaker to catch your attention before talking to you
- Ask speaker to face you when talking
- Ask speaker not to shout
- Ask partner/friend to introduce/summarize/give gist of the topic of conversation, especially if you are joining a group of people
- Ask partner/friend to rephrase/repeat a misheard or difficult sentence
- Repeat sentence/phrase back to speaker/ask a reversed question to confirm details
- Give feedback – nod, smile, frown, look puzzled
- Tell others that you are 'hard-of-hearing'/having difficulty.

Tactics involving manipulating the physical environment

- Make sure that there is enough light falling on the face of the speaker
- Make sure that there is nothing obscuring the speaker's face
- Move closer to the speaker; do not have them shout from another room
- Try to talk in a quiet room – get away from noise, shut doors
- Turn down interfering noise from TV/radio/household appliances

2   Field, D.L. and Haggard, M.P., 'Knowledge of Hearing Tactics: (1) Assessment by questionnaire and inventory.' *British Journal of Audiology* 1989, 23, 349–354 with the permission of Dr Haggard.

- Sit close to the front or near the loudspeaker in church/theatre/hall
- Adjust tuning or tone control of radio/TV/record player (relatively more treble for talk programmes, more base for music); reduce volume to prevent distortion
- Turn 'good' side towards source of speech; have speaker sitting/standing on side of 'good' ear
- Have soft furnishings (think carpets, heavy curtains).

Tactics involving observation

- Use visual cues; watch lips/face of the speaker
- Take note of the context, facial expressions and gestures
- Fill in the gaps or guess parts of the conversation based on the knowledge of the speaker, the topic or the last thing they or you said
- Keep calm/unflustered, be patient.

Helping a Hearing Impaired Person to Communicate and Lipread

The Sympathetic Hearing Scheme aims to help deaf and hard of hearing people to live easier lives. The scheme utilizes the World Deaf Symbol shown in Figure 8.1

Figure 8.1. The World Deaf Symbol

Eventually it is hoped that the symbol will be displayed wherever someone is available to serve a deaf or hard of hearing person on request. The Scheme has prepared the following guidelines to assist anyone when dealing with a hearing impaired person.

- Do *not* shout. It is a common reaction but it does not help and only causes embarrassment.

- Speak slowly and clearly, but do not exaggerate your facial movements or distort your face.

- Try to face the light as well as the person to whom you are speaking.

- Cut out as much background noise as possible.

- Do not smoke, eat or do anything else that involves putting your hand in front of your face. Lipreaders must be able to see your mouth.

- Use plain language. Many words look the same to lipreaders. The more common the word the better.

- If you are not immediately understood, try rephrasing what you are saying.

- Write things down if you think it necessary. Again it is easier for you both if you use common and quite short words.

- If a deaf customer is accompanied by a hearing friend, address what you are saying to the customer. The friend will still be able to follow and help if needed.

The following additional guidelines may be added to the above.

- Stand or sit about four to five feet from the person to whom you are speaking. Experiment until you find out how near you need to be to make his hearing aid and lipreading useful.

- Don't let the person bluff and get away with it.

- Don't say the word over and over again. Many words are difficult to see on the lips. Change the wording and try again. For example, if he doesn't understand when you say 'Can I see your Mum?' try 'Can I talk to your Mother?'

- Watch for signs of fatigue.

- If his attention wanders attract it in an inconspicuous way.

- Be patient with mistakes. *Never* show signs of annoyance.

Supplementing Lipreading

Given average natural ability, application and confidence there is no reason why a level of lipreading adequate for most circumstances cannot be achieved. In practice the uncertainties of lipreading can be partially overcome by Sign Language and what are termed Manually Coded English Systems which contrive to provide a visual representation of spoken languages.

(1) Sign Language

Signing is usually disliked and avoided by people who have acquired a severe hearing loss in later life. This aversion is partly due to the desire to avoid appearing abnormal. The aversion, while understandable is somewhat irrational. If we go to a foreign country and have difficulty with the language we are not afraid to sign our wants or questions. There are three main approaches to sign language: Sign Language (BSL), Signs Supporting English (SSE) and Finger Spelling.

British Sign Language

This is the language of the Deaf Community in Britain which numbers about 50,000 people. It is, therefore, claimed to be Britain's fourth language in terms of usage ranking after the dominant English language, Welsh, spoken by 500,000 people and Scottish Gaelic which has about 80,000 users. Brennan[3] has described BSL as a 'visual gestural language' and argues that both elements of this description are crucial to an understanding of this communication system. It is a language which is perceived by the eye and it therefore exploits forms of patterning which are easily visible. It is produced in the form of gestures which occur in space.

Signs may be classified into several categories. *Natural* signs may have some analogy to the idea suggested but not described, for example head resting on palms together, for 'go to sleep'. *Derivative* signs may be developed from some root idea such as the sign for girl or woman, where the upright forefinger is moved across the mouth to convey the idea of a beardless person. In contrast the sign for man is made by bringing the fist down the face to indicate a beard. *Indicative* signs are made by pointing to the object intended. Some signs such as thumbs up for 'good' have no analogous associations. Many people with normal hearing endeavour to obtain varying levels of proficiency in BSL to enable them to communicate with people for whom BSL is their first language. *A Sign Language and Interpreting Information Pack*, available free from the RNID, gives details of a range of training videos and books relating to BSL. The latter include a *Dictionary of British Sign Language/English* compiled by the Deaf Studies Research Unit of Durham University and issued by the British Deaf Association. The Council for the Advancement of Communication with Deaf Persons was founded in 1980. the main aims of the CACDP are:

(1) to promote training and conduct examinations in communication skills

---

3   'Grammatical Processes in British Sign Language.' In B. Well, J. Kyle and Deuchove *Perspectives in British Sign Language and Deafness.* Croom Helm, 1981, p.120.

(2) to maintain and administer a Register of Interpreters.

Signs Supporting English

Unlike BSL this is not an independent language but combines signs from BSL with spoken English. It is, therefore, a mixture of two languages, English and BSL. The grammar is mainly English but lipreaders are assisted by the addition of BSL sign language or other features.

Finger Spelling

To represent specific English words or to spell out proper names, foreign and new, perhaps technical words, that currently have no agreed sign, signers use the manual alphabet as shown in Figure 8.2.

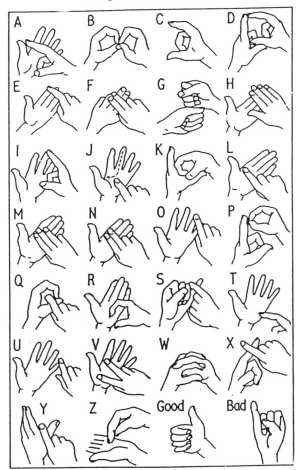

Figure 8.2. Manual alphabet

Finger spelling simply involves positioning the fingers in 26 different positions to represent the 26 letters of the alphabet. The five vowels are indicated by touching with the right forefinger, the tip of the left thumb for A, the first finger for E, the middle one for I, the next for O and the little finger for U. For consonants the position of the fingers roughly forms the shape of the printed letter.

Finger spelling can be used in conjunction with speech, lipreading, amplification and with other manual methods.

Finger spelling can be quickly learned but regular practice over a considerable time is needed before rapid finger spelling can be read. When this proficiency has been attained, finger spelling is about twice as rapid as writing.

Since finger spelling is the easiest means of communicating with severely hearing impaired persons, the following hints are given:

- Hold the left hand with the palm towards the person you are addressing.

- Keep the fingers of the left had outspread, making them easier to see.

- Normally the finger speller does not pause for punctuation or capitals; words run together with a space between them. At first, however, it is easier to read if the finger speller makes a break at the end of each word.

- Special care is needed with vowels since the wrong touch of a vowel finger can completely alter a word, eg *bear* to *beer*.

Manually Coded English Systems

Two such systems, the Danish Mouth–Hand System and Cued Speech aim to increase the accuracy of speech reading and reduce the strain involved by enabling speech sounds to be more easily recognized. These systems are particularly useful with traumatically deafened persons or where one member of a family has a severe hearing loss which cannot be overcome with a hearing aid.

The Danish Mouth–Hand System

This was devised in 1902 by George Forchhammer, a Danish teacher of the deaf. Forchhammer recognized that only thirty per cent of all Danish speech sounds could be identified with reasonable certainty. As the vowels belong to this thirty per cent it is clear that the main difficulties are with the consonants. As indicated earlier, the sounds *p*, *b* and *m* are identical on the lips and the correct word has to be determined from the context in which it is used. In the English version of Forchhammer's system eighteen symbols are used to represent twenty-two consonant sounds. Separate signs are provided for *p*, *b* and *m* so that guesswork is eliminated.

As shown by Figure 8.3 the various movements are made by one hand positioned under the chin and close to the chest of the speaker.

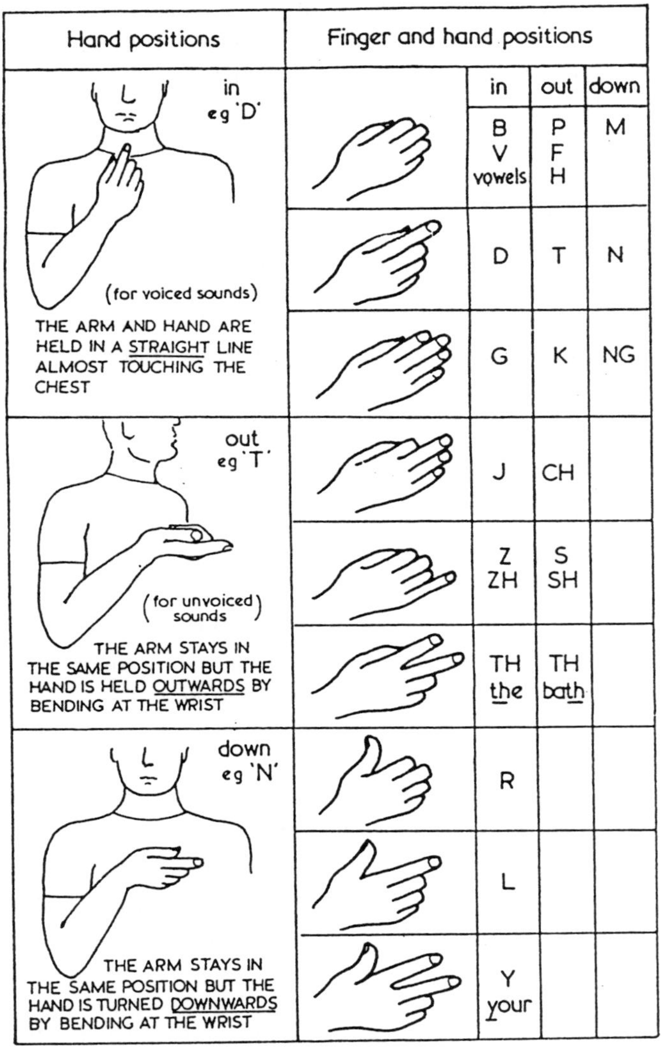

Hand positions	Finger and hand positions			
		in	out	down
L in eg 'D' (for voiced sounds) THE ARM AND HAND ARE HELD IN A STRAIGHT LINE ALMOST TOUCHING THE CHEST		B V vowels	P F H	M
		D	T	N
		G	K	NG
L out eg 'T' (for unvoiced) sounds THE ARM STAYS IN THE SAME POSITION BUT THE HAND IS HELD OUTWARDS BY BENDING AT THE WRIST		J	CH	
		Z ZH	S SH	
		TH the	TH bath	
L down eg 'N' THE ARM STAYS IN THE SAME POSITION BUT THE HAND IS TURNED DOWNWARDS BY BENDING AT THE WRIST		R		
		L		
		Y your		

Figure 8.3. The Danish Mouth–Hand System

This ensures that both the speaker's mouth and hand can be clearly seen by the lipreader while the hand movements are relatively inconspicuous. It is estimated that the system can be learnt in about twelve hours and used with reasonable confidence after eight hours further practice. In the UK this system has not achieved the popularity of Cued Speech.

Cued Speech

Cued speech has some similarities to the Danish Mouth–Hand System. Both systems aim to support or supplement lipreading, are basically phonetic and involve hand and mouth movements used together. In neither system can a sound be read from the hand movements only. While the Mouth–Hand system was primarily designed for adults, cued speech was invented (in 1966) to assist deaf or deafened children to acquire the language they have never heard and to develop pronunciation and rhythmic speech. Accordingly cued speech provides signals for *all the speech sounds used in normal conversation.*

As shown in Figure 8.3 cues consist of a set of hand signals to be synchronized with lip movements. These cues differ from signs in that the latter are pictorial representations of objects or ideas; cues provide comprehensive and precise oral information. Cued speech also provides an alternative to finger spelling.

In cued speech, the four positions represent the vowels and the right hand shapes the consonants. It is claimed that this combination provides a one-to-one visible representation of the syllables and phonemes of spoken language. Since the lipreader has to recall which of twenty-four consonant shapes are associated with a particular hand shape, considerable practice is required and, in this respect, cued speech is more complex than the Danish Mouth–Hand System.

Auditory Training

The broad aim of auditory training or retraining is to enable a person with impaired hearing to make the best possible use of any residual hearing. Auditory training has been somewhat narrowly defined as 'a procedure aimed at improving awareness, discrimination and retention of speech sounds'.

Whether you or any hearing impaired person you know would benefit from auditory training can be determined only after considering the data obtained from audiometric tests and other information. Audiometric tests include those for pure tones and speech described earlier in this book. Other factors include the cause, nature and extent of hearing loss; the age of onset and duration of the impairment; the degree to which the person concerned can compensate for his hearing loss by means of a suitable aid. Where, as with cases of pure conductive loss, a hearing aid enables the user to cope satisfactorily with all normal situations, auditory training is not required. Conversely, where someone has a mixed or sensorineural loss giving rise to discrimination difficulties, auditory training might be beneficial. Probably the best rough and ready indication for or against the usefulness of auditory training to an individual is that person's ability to discriminate between speech sounds.

Auditory training covers many components. Most auditory training pro-grammes would include:

Hearing aid orientation. Overcoming resistance or apathy towards hearing aid use; advice on the advantages and limitations of hearing aids; setting the controls for maximum benefit; minor repairs and adjustments; the use of the aid outside, in noisy surroundings and in group situations. Assisting elderly persons to make the best use of an aid.

Listening practice. This may take several forms. Persons with a significant hearing loss tend to listen selectively, thereby giving the impression that they 'can hear when they want to'. People with normal hearing often fail to recognize that the tension and anxiety experienced by a hearing impaired person is very fatiguing and that such selective listening is a conscious or unconscious way of conserving energy. Listening practice may attempt to improve speech discrimination under both favourable and unfavourable conditions. It may try to improve a person's capacity to localize sounds. An enhanced awareness of listening behaviour on the part of a hearing impaired person may help to avoid annoyance to others because of seeming inattention.

Sound location. Helping persons with a severe loss in one ear and a moderate loss in the other to locate the direction of a sound source.

Noise tolerance. Advice as to how noise may be constructively dealt with. This is especially important for people with 'recruitment' problems, when increased volume provided by a hearing aid can lead to diminished discrimination.

Speech conservation and improvement. Helping severely deafened adults with long-standing impairments that have resulted in speech and voice deterioration.

A new dimension has been added to the importance of auditory training by the extensive post operative rehabilitation required by cochlear implant users.

Auditory training, as one audiologist, Markides, has pointed out, involves systematic and persistent practice under the direction of a professional therapist with the end result depending primarily on the qualities of the therapist combined with attributes relating to the individual hearing impaired person, including motivation; co-operation with the therapist; age; intelligence; systematic practice; habilitation; understanding of the basic principles involved and the degree, pattern and type of hearing impairment.

Although facilities for auditory training might be expected to improve as the number of hearing therapists in post increases, the provision of such training is, at the time of writing (1995) patchy and in some areas non-existent. If, in the opinion of your otologist, you would benefit from auditory training but no facilities are available locally, you should raise the matter with your health authority or the RNID or BAHOH.

9

Employment, Hospitalization and Family Relationships

Apart from the psychological factors mentioned in Chapter 6 hearing loss, according to its severity, causes a chain reaction of problems affecting in some degrees every facet of life. Three important aspects of hearing loss are employment, hospitalization and family relationships.

Employment

The handicapping effects of hearing loss on employment are a major source of anxiety for persons who become hard of hearing or deafened between the ages of school leaving and retirement. A study in 1982 by Thomas, Lamont and Harris[1] of 88 adults of employment age with an acquired hearing loss greater than 60 dB indicates that while the respondents were not then likely to be unemployed because of the hearing loss, they were experiencing difficulty in coping at work for a variety of reasons, categorized under five headings:

(1) Dealing with people other than colleagues.

(2) Formal work relations.

(3) Job proficiency.

(4) Social relationships.

(5) Loss of status.

It was evident that a majority of respondents had problems with the telephone and dealing with people other than colleagues (Section 1) and a significant number had experienced either job loss or loss of status.

Hearing loss may also affect ability to participate in group discussions while restricted social relationships at work and can cause feelings of isolation, inadequacy and marginality. Employment seeking also becomes more difficult because of communication problems at interviews and the sometimes negative

---

1   Thomas, Lamont and Harris (1982) 'Problems encountered at work by people with severe acquiria hearing loss.' *British Journal of Audiology 16*, pp.39–43.

or unsympathetic attitudes of employers. A hard of hearing or deafened person may experience a dichotomy of relief at having secured or retained employment and frustration at the restrictions imposed by the disability or opportunities for advancement.

When considering the problems of employment consequent on hearing loss three important factors must be considered.

First, the extent to which a person is handicapped depends on the nature of the job. The results of a survey of the policies and practices of employers relating to people with disabilities published by the Department of Employment in 1990 reported that the number of employers who rated 'good hearing' as important was 76 per cent for management positions but only 65 per cent and 53 per cent for 'skilled manual' and other manual jobs respectively. Management jobs clearly involve considerable verbal communication with individuals and groups both from within the organization and those who are not immediate colleagues. In some jobs good hearing for the purpose of monitoring a machine or process is essential. More often, the real danger is that hearing loss may constitute a safety hazard. According to Common Law an employer has a duty to provide both safe conditions of work and safe fellow workers. In some circumstances the employment of a person with a significant hearing loss might be held to constitute a breach of this duty. Safety is also governed by the Health and Safety at Work Act 1974 which provides that 'It shall be the duty of every employer to ensure, so far as is reasonably practicable, the health, safety and welfare at work of all his employees'. This Act also imposes a statutory duty on the employee 'to co-operate with his employer or any other person' in carrying out safety legislation. This means that if your hearing loss constitutes a safety hazard you must report it to the employer so that he can make appropriate safety arrangements. If, as a result of non-disclosure, an accident occurs, some liability might accrue to you. Any compensation for industrial injury might also be reduced if an element of contributory negligence on your part can be proved.

When safety hazards can be overcome, even a severe hearing loss might be a comparatively minor occupational handicap. This is especially so when only a small amount of social interaction is involved and the use of the telephone is not normally required.

Second, in recent years there has been an enhanced understanding of disability including hearing loss especially on the part of larger employers. Currently (1995) approaching one thousand employers have committed themselves to using the disability symbol shown in Figure 9.1.

Symbol users are committed to:

o interviewing all applicants with a disability who meet the minimum criteria for a job vacancy and considering them on these abilities o making every effort when employees become disabled to ensure they stay in employment

o taking action to ensure that key employees develop the awareness of disability to make the employer's commitment work

o reviewing the above commitments each year to ascertain what has been achieved, planning ways to improve on them and informing all employees about progress and future plans.

Figure 9.1. The Disability Symbol

Section 235 of the Companies Act 1985 requires all employers employing on average more than 250 people to include in the directors' report a statement of the policy applied during the previous year for giving full consideration to people with disabilities applying for jobs.

Some of the largest employers in Great Britain are affiliated to the Employers Forum for Disability which is concerned with the promotion of training and employment for people with disabilities. these developments are important. In the last analysis it is the attitudes of your employer and colleagues which determine whether or not you can cope successfully with the employment problems ensuing from hearing loss.

Third, technology has done much to mitigate the degree to which hearing impairment constitutes an occupational handicap. Improvements to hearing aids have been discussed earlier in this book. A number of ingenious devices have been developed to help people with a hearing loss to cope. There are, for example, amplifying stethoscopes for hard of hearing doctors. Palantyne machines, originally developed by Dr Alan Newall (then of Southampton University) for use by Jack Ashley MP at the House of Commons can enable persons with a profound hearing loss to follow lectures and meetings. Details of Palantyne machines can be obtained from Sound Advantage. Text-telephones (Minicoms) and services such as Typetalk can help deafened people communicate by telephone. Typetalk enables a deaf user to send a message by means of a Minicom or Qwertyphone. The operator at the Typetalk Exchange relays the message to the hearing receiver who uses a normal telephone. The hearing person uses the telephone to reply and in the Type talk Exchange the message is relayed to the deaf person who receives it on a Minicom. Video phones will further assist hearing impaired telephone users. Amplified handsets and earpieces can help those who are hard of hearing. Electronic mail and Fax can sometimes obviate the need for telephone messages, flashing lights can convey warning signals, and do not let these technological wonders cause you to overlook toe possibilities of a pad and pencil.

Ultimately, however, coping with the handicaps consequent on hearing loss requires a high capacity for self-help and sometimes assistance from Government and voluntary services.

Self-help in Employment

When hearing interferes significantly with employment the first step is to undertake a realistic self-assessment along the following lines:

(1) What is the expected duration of your future working life?

If hearing loss acquires a handicapping proportion at, say, the age of 40, you will have left a maximum working life of from 15 to 25 years. Some retraining either for advancement or for work in which the disability is less of a handicap may be advisable. At the age of 55, however, the emphasis should be either on retraining for your present job, or perhaps, early retirement.

(2) Is the hearing loss progressive and irreversible?

If so try to estimate the employment problems likely to be encountered in ten years; time. You may, for example, be able to use the telephone now but in ten years assistance will be required. Otologists do not always recognize the importance of providing a prognosis which, while avoiding unnecessary anxiety, enables a hearing impaired person to plan for the future.

(3) Is your present job likely to make your hearing worse or cause other physical symptoms or mental strain?

Excessive noise exposure may cause hearing to deteriorate further. Meetings, discussions and telephone conversations may cause feelings of strain, inadequacy and loss of confidence. In such cases change to a less demanding job may be beneficial.

(4) How can your existing qualifications, skills, experience and vocational interests be constructively used?

Consideration of these factors may indicate opportunities for self-employment retraining or transferring to other work in the same organization. Examples of successful transfers include the deafened bank clerk who moved from counter work to accounts supervision and the librarian who became an archivist.

(5) How can you be helped to cope in your present job?

Even severely disabled persons can cope with responsible jobs on a team basis. A good colleague or personal assistant who can act as the ears, eyes and sometimes voice of an executive is invaluable. Such an aide can receive and transmit telephone messages, take notes at meetings and bring important matters to your attention. The use of hearing tactics and the various devices of the technology described earlier can solve many problems.

(6) What are your priorities?

These change throughout life. Younger people may wish to obtain promotion notwithstanding a handicap; people in middle life may wish to keep the job for economic reasons; as you grow older a less frenetic life and the opportunity to enjoy hobbies and home may become paramount.

An evaluation such as the above will suggest a least six possible options regarding employment according to your age, aptitudes, abilities and present and likely future hearing loss. You may attempt to keep and possibly progress in your existing job; transfer to alternative work with the same employer; seek less demanding or more responsible work elsewhere; retrain for new work; become self-employed or, where appropriate, take early retirement.

Self-employment and early retirement raise so many individual issues that it is impracticable to discuss such options here. Most people with a significant hearing loss will find that the most prudent course is to stay with their present employer. Employers are often more ready to assist existing employees than make similar concessions or assistance available to new workers. Furthermore, both employee and colleagues gradually acquire an understanding of hearing impairment and its consequences. The extent to which they do this depends largely on you. Do not attempt to hide your handicap or bluff your way through; do not be too proud to seek help; inform your employer how you may be helped by environmental and other devices and emphasize what you *can* do rather than your limitations.

Help from Government and Voluntary Sources

The following suggestions indicate how you can take positive steps to obtain or retain employment by using the assistance provided by statutory and voluntary agencies.

Register under the Disabled Persons Employment Acts

This Register was set up by the Disabled Persons (Employment) Act 1944 which defined a disabled person for employment purposes as 'a person who, on account of injury, disease or congenital deformity, is substantially handicapped in obtaining or keeping employment or in undertaking work on his own account; of a kind which apart from that injury, disease or deformity, would be suited to his age, experience or qualifications'.

Difficulties in enforcing the provisions of the Act have been encountered and for that reason many people do not bother to register. Registration does, however, provide the advantage that you are covered by the protection afforded by the Act, which provides that: 'Employers with 20 or more employees must employ a quote of registered disabled people'. It is, however, likely that this Act will be repeated when the Disability Discrimination Bill currently (1995) before Parliament is passed into law probably in 1996.

- It is an offence for an employer who is below the quota to engage anyone other than a registered disabled person without first obtaining a permit to do so from the Job Centre.
- It is an offence to make a registered disabled person redundant without reasonable cause if the employer is either already below quota or would fall below quota as a result.

The Job Centre can refuse to issue a permit if it can be shown that an employer is discriminating against disabled applicants.

Make contact with your Disability Employment Adviser

The Disability Employment Adviser (DEA) based at your Job Centre is part of a team of disability specialists in the *Placing, Assessment and Counselling Team* known as the *PACT*.

The DEA's functions is to work with disabled people who need extra help to assess these abilities and agree with them an action plan to find the right job. The DEA can advise on

- jobs with interested employers
- how best to find the most suitable jobs or training
- the *Job Introduction Scheme* – which offers a chance to try out a job for an introductory period
- individual practical help using *Access to Work*
- work preparation including job trial with an employer
- the change to try out useful equipment
- registering as disabled

o   training to update and gain new skills – Training for Work

o   work opportunities under the *Sheltered Placement Scheme* or jobs in sheltered workshops run by local authorities, voluntary organizations and Remploy.

The Access to Work scheme which began on 6 June 1994 is for unemployed; employed and self-employed disabled people who need help to get a job, keep a job or make progress in their career. Registration under the Disabled Persons Employment Act is not obligatory. Each applicant will be able to get help to the value of up to £21,000 over five years, although most people need much less. The Access to Work Scheme can, for example, pay for a communicator for people who are deaf or have a hearing impairment or for the special technological equipment mentioned earlier in this chapter.

If you require help with self-employment or training it is also useful to contact your nearest Training and Enterprise Council (TEC) which, *inter alia*, will offer information and support services for disabled people contemplating setting up in business. Specialist help in training, such as communicators for people with a profound hearing loss, may also be given.

Ascertain what help is available from voluntary agencies

The RNID has published a *Good Practice Guide* to help employers with deaf applicants and employees.

The National Association for Deafened People will put deafened people with employment problems in touch with other members who can provide practical advice based on experience. *SKILL (The National Bureau for Students with Disabilities)* may be able to offer advice on training grants and opportunities. The *Disabled Graduates Career Information Service* keeps a register of disabled graduate job seekers. The *Disabled Living Foundation* has an excellent publication *How to Get Equipment for Disability*. A copy may be available in your local reference library. The *Employers Forum on Disability* has been referred to above. The *Royal Association for Disability and Rehabilitation (RADAR)* may also be worth contacting.

Hospitalization

When you have a hearing loss, going to hospital either as in in-patient or out-patient can be a traumatic experience. You will cope best if from the outset you resolve not to attempt to bluff your way through and, so far as possible, control rather than be controlled by the situation. Some common situations and strategies for coping are indicated overleaf:

Situation and problem	*Possible solution*
Reception: noisy environment: failure to hear your name when called.	Tell the receptionist that you are 'deaf'. (Receptionists are unlikely to distinguish between deaf or hard of hearing.) Ask the receptionist either to signal to you or come over and tell you when you are wanted. Take a friend with you to act as your ears and eyes. Ask the receptionist to state that you are 'deaf' on all your records.
Consultation: Doctors may speak quickly and turn their heads away. Conditions may make lipreading' difficult (e.g. ophthalmic examinations in dark surroundings or silence). Examinations where you have difficulty in seeing the doctor's face.	Remind the doctor that you 'do not hear well'. Never say 'yes' or 'nod' your head if you do not understand whar he has said. Ask doctor to speak slowly or write down questions on a pad. For ophthalmic tests or examinations ask the opthalmologist to use your right thumb as a joy stick or move it in the direction you are required to look. One advantage of behind the ear aids is that you can keep your aid on when your clothes are off.
Radiology: Often dark room; flat surface on which to lie; radiology staff sometimes give instructions from another room.	Tell the clinician that you have difficulty in hearing and cannot lipread in the dark. Ask whether it is necessary for you to remove your hearing aid. (This will be essential for head X rays or CT and CAT brain scans.) Cochlear implants may require to be disconnected.
Admissions to hospital:	Ask about the possibilities of your own room where it may be easier to discriminate speech than in a noisy ward. Inform the nurses of your deafness. If one ear is better than the other ask doctor and nurses to speak to you from your better side. Ensure that a note about your hearing is on all your records.

Operations: Inability to lipread anyone wearing a surgical mask; need to remove hearing aid.

Ask the anaesthetist to give instructions before pulling on the mask at what point your hearing aid must be removed and when, after the operation, you can put it back on.

Some general points:

o Remember that you have a right to expect patience, courtesy, a reasonable response to your requests and an explanation of the treatments you are to receive or undergo.

o Keep a sense of humour.

o Ask doctors to write down instructions for medication and other important matters.

o Repeat oral instructions to the doctor to ensure that you have understood them.

o When entering hospital ensure that you have:

   o A supply of hearing aid batteries to last for your expected stay.

   o Spare plastic tubing.

   o Accessories for the cleaning and 'plumbing' of your aid.

   o A note pad and pencil for communication purposes or even better a communicator for transmitting and receiving messages on a one-to-one basis.

Family Relationships

Most research on the effects of severe hearing impairment on family relationships tends to be reported in academic journals to which the general reader is unlikely to have access. The best British study is *Words Apart* by Jones, Kyle and Wood (1987). It has been reported from the USA that the incidence of divorce where both partners are severely deaf is lower than for the general population. Probably the shared knowledge of the consequences of the disability provides mutual understanding. There will also, normally, be fewer outside contacts.

Where, however, either husband or wife is handicapped to the extent that even with a hearing aid normal communication becomes difficulty, the effect on the other partner and on members of the family can be significant. The reasons why relationships may be affected are diverse and must be faced.

Hearing loss restricts the social intercourse of family life. The basis of the family is community. Community in turn depends on communication. Especially at meal times the exchange of news, experiences, gossip and humour helps to cement a bond between family members. When one member is unable to join in he or she may experience feelings of isolation or rejection. Conversely, the hearing members may feel guilt or embarrassment at 'leaving out' the person with hearing difficulties. A marriage may become strained when the whispered intimacies that mean so much between husband and wife become impossible.

Inability to hear can lead to frustration and irritability both for the person affected and other family members. The frustration of trying to transmit and receive messages, the necessity of repeating an item several times or of acting as a second pair of ears may cause patience to wear thin. When hearing members of a household are exposed to the stress of a television with the volume switch at a high level it is not surprising that irritation arises.

Hearing impairment may make it difficult for partners to develop or maintain common interests. The hearing partner, for example, may enjoy dancing or making new friends. The hearing impaired partner may find dancing difficult and meeting strangers a strain – so he or she will either go to such activities under protest or stay at home. The writer knows of a wife whose husband appeared to be uninterested because he would not attend parent–teacher meetings when in reality he was afraid of not hearing what was said and appearing stupid. Another lady resented the unwillingness of her husband to accompany her to church even though he told her repeatedly that the reason was that he could hear little of the service.

Hearing impairment may cause a reversal of traditional roles. Thus, where the mother is severely hard of hearing it will be the father who will have to listen for the children and care for them in the night. One hard-of-hearing man remarked 'If we have burglars my wife will have to get up, because I shan't hear them'. Another deafened man resented the fact that his children took their school homework to their mother instead of him because they had difficulty in making him understand what was required. A hearing-impaired person's ego can often be bruised by feelings of uselessness, inadequacy and inferiority.

Hearing impairment may give rise to conflict because of the misunderstanding of requests or instructions. Frequently someone who is hard of hearing may protest that he has 'never been told' to which the counter-accusation is that 'you didn't pay attention'. This misunderstanding can be enhanced by the insensitivity of children and adolescents. Jones, Kyle and Wood quote the nineteen-year-old son of a hard-of-hearing mother as an example of the viewpoint of a hearing adolescent.

> 'You have to get used to telling her half-a-dozen times. I lose my temper after two or three times and walk out. We're not the sort to talk anyway,

there's nothing important to talk about, so it doesn't matter – I treat my room like a bed sit.'[2]

How these possible causes of friction and breakdown are resolved within a marriage depends primarily on the maturity, understanding, and affection of the partners themselves. One man answered the assertion that his severely hard-of-hearing wife 'must be a burden by quoting a saying of Thomas-a- Kempis, 'Love taketh a burden and maketh it no burden'. At the other extreme is the experience of a Danish lady.

> 'Marriage problems? My answer to this must be "yes". To me it was simply a catastrophe. The husband thought it was horrible to have a hearing impaired wife. He thought I was a millstone round his neck. When I realized I could sink no deeper or get no worse I had my divorce.'

There is a great need for short intensive courses to help those with normal hearing to become orientated to the problems of the severely hard of hearing and deafened. Such help is provided by the Link Centre for Deafened People, Eastbourne and the Birmingham Resource Centre for Deafened People.

The Link Centre provides a one week residential course aimed at helping people handicapped by sudden severe or total deafness together with members of their family. For those attending it provides a tailor made programme which may include intensive help with communication skills, employment questions, demonstration of equipment, family relationships and similar problems. Part or all of the cost of the course may be met by the Social Service Department of the local authority within which course members reside.

The Birmingham Resource Centre for Deafened People works within the NHS and is funded by health authorities in the area. The Centre specializes in the care of people who have lost most or all of their hearing and is staffed by a multi-disciplinary team of therapists who carefully assess and plan a rehabilitation programme appropriate to the needs of each person. Assessment takes place at the Centre and, for some aspects, at the Queen Elizabeth Hospital, Birmingham. Deafened people attend with their families for a number of assessment sessions. Rehabilitation is approached in three interdependent ways: improving hearing and sound perception; improving basic communication skills; aiding adjustment to the emotional and social effects of severe hearing loss.

Factors that help in ensuring that a hearing loss affecting one member has the minimum effect on family relationships include the following:

---

2   Jones, Kyle and Wood (1987) *Words Apart*. Tavistock Publication, p.172

Emotional security

A hearing-impaired person who is lived, respected and accepted will be less likely to succumb to feelings of inferiority and hopelessness and the tension from frustration will be less.

A positive self-concept

The person with hearing loss must be encouraged to play as full a part as possible in home activities. He or she must be consulted on domestic decisions and never by-passed because of communication difficulties. The 'does he take sugar in his tea?' syndrome must be carefully avoided.

Communication Skills

Both the person concerned and members of the family should do everything possible to learn lipreading or such aids to lipreading as Cued Speech or the Danish Mouth–Hand System. The greater the mastery of these skills, the more the person with a hearing loss will be included in the family circle.

Use of Environmental Aids

Such aids can greatly reduce tension, especially in relation to door bells and the television.

Finally, as suggested in Chapter 5, the person with the hearing loss must also be prepared to develop empathy. Such empathy will help stifle self-pity and an awareness that hearing loss causes problems not only for himself or herself but for all members of the family. This empathy may also recognize the need for relaxation on the part of hearing members of the family. Jones, Kyle and Wood[3] instance the need for relaxation expressed by the hearing wife of a man who also had a visual handicap.

> 'You need somewhere you can go and scream about it and then come back for another month. You've got to get out, like with small children, you can get it out of proportion, you need the peace and quiet of getting away and giving your ears a rest – I take the dog out.'

People with a hearing loss need to be understood; they also need to understand.

---

3   Jones, Kyle and Wood *ibid.*

10

Statutory and Voluntary Services for People with Impaired Hearing

This final chapter aims to give an outline of the scope and development of statutory services of relevance to people with a hearing loss and the main voluntary organizations associated with hearing impairment.

Statutory Services
The National Assistance Acts 1948 and later

Statutory recognition was given for the first time to hearing impaired adults by Section 29 of the National Assistance Act 1948. This Act empowered the then County and County Borough Councils to make arrangements for:

> 'Promoting the welfare of persons who are blind, deaf or dumb and other persons who are substantially handicapped by illness, injury and congenital deformity and such other disabilities as may be described by the Minister.'

It is important to notice that the wording is dear *or* dumb, not deaf and dumb. The word 'deaf' was therefore a generic term covering all categories of hearing loss. The term 'dumb' is, of course, now archaic and should never be used. It has not, however, been amended in the above definition.

In 1948 local authority provisions for categories of handicapped persons other than those who were blind was only discretionary. It was not until 1960 that the Minister made the exercise of their powers with reference to the 'deaf or dumb' mandatory on the local authorities.

Meanwhile, in 1951, the Minister had issued a circular (32/51) setting out a model scheme detailing the services that a local authority must or might provide for the deaf or dumb. The writer understands that this circular has not been withdrawn (1995) and so it indicates the kind of services that a person with a hearing loss irrespective of its severity, can enquire about. The model scheme was applicable to both the deaf and the hard of hearing. The Minister stated that he would be reluctant to approve schemes submitted by local authorities unless these included arrangements for the following services:

'Assistance to deal or dumb persons to overcome the effects of these disabilities and to obtain treatment. An advisory service on personal and other problems. Encouragement to deaf or dumb persons to take part in social activities. Visitation by voluntary workers.'

In the Minister's model scheme, the following services *could* be provided:

o provision of practical assistance in the home

o provision of assistance in obtaining wireless, library and other recreational facilities

o provision of lectures, games and other recreational facilities in social centres by way of outings, etc.

o provision of travelling facilities so that deaf or dumb persons can take advantage of the service provided

o helping deaf or dumb persons to take holidays or holiday homes

o provision of social centres or holiday homes.

As indicated in the Introduction to this book, circular 32/51 required local authorities to keep a register of handicapped persons who applied for help. The purpose of the register was to enable the authority to have some idea of the numbers of people under each class for whom provision needs to be made. For the hearing impaired this register as raised in 1961 was subdivided into three categories according to the person's *present* condition and needs rather than according to the *origin* of the disability. The three categories, defined in the Introduction are (1) Deaf without speech; (2) Deaf with speech; (3) the hard of hearing.

Since the passing of the Local Authority Social Services Act 1968 most local authorities have appointed their own welfare officers for the hearing impaired and have taken over responsibility for services to the 'deaf' either wholly or in part from the local voluntary societies for the deaf by whom such services were pioneered and provided for over 100 years. Some local authorities still carry out their responsibilities to the hearing impaired by using the services of a voluntary society under a full or partial agency agreement. The Act, while overtaken by later legislation, is still in force and may be regarded as the cornerstone of legislation in the field of disability.

The Hearing Aid Council Act 1968

Established the Hearing Aid Council 'to register persons engaged in the supply of hearing aids, to advise in the training of persons engaged in such business and to regulate trade practices; and for persons connected therewith'.

The Chronically Sick and Disabled Persons Act 1970

Hearing impaired people may be eligible for assistance under the terms of this Act, Section 2 of which requires a local authority Social Services Department, when it is satisfied of the necessity to do so, to provide or give assistance to handicapped persons to obtain any or all of the following services: practical assistance in the home; wireless; television, library or similar recreational facilities in the home; recreational or travelling facilities outside the home and assistance in taking advantage of educational facilities; support in minimizing the social and personal consequences of illness and disability to individuals and families; assistance in carrying out adaptations to the home or provision of additional facilities to secure greater safety, comfort or convenience; facilitating the taking of holidays; meals at home or elsewhere, telephone and any special equipment necessary for its use.

Sections 1 and 2 of the Act also state that 'It shall be the duty of every local authority having functions under Section 29 of the National Assistance Act to inform themselves of the number of persons to whom that section applies in their area and of the need for the making by the authority of arrangements under that section for such persons.'

The Act has been only partially successful, due to under-funding.

The legislation has, however, applications to the needs of people with hearing impairments. 'Telephone and other equipment' can include Minicoms, amplified telephones and other associated equipment. Only telephone and television are explicitly mentioned under daily living equipment. The provision of environmental aids for people with hearing loss is, however, covered by the term 'facilities'.

The National Health Service Act 1977

Covers the provision of hearing aids by the health service under the duty to provide 'medical services'.

The Disabled Persons (Services, Consultation and Representation) Act 1986

Gives disabled persons the right to appoint authorized representatives (e.g. a friend, advocate or spokesperson) when negotiating with social services departments. Section 4 states that when requested by a disabled person, carer or authorized representative, the local authority must assess his or her needs for services under the 1970 Local Authority Social Services Act. Services might include environmental aids and adaptations, minicoms, and home helps.

The National Health Service and Community Care Act 1990

Among other matters this Act makes further provision concerning the arrangements for accommodation and other welfare services by local authorities and the powers of the Secretary of State regarding the social services functions of such authorities. Section 47 provides that local authorities shall assess the needs of any person in respect of where it appears that they may provide or arrange for the provision of such services. The authority shall then decide whether the needs assessed call for the provision of local authority services. If it appears to the local authority that an applicant is a disabled person it may proceed to make a decision with regard to the services required as mentioned in Section 4 of the Disabled Persons (Services, Consultation and Representation) Act 1986 without the disabled person requesting assessment under the Act.

Social Security Benefits

Social Security provision is subject to frequent change. Details of current entitlements may be obtained by telephoning the Benefits Agency on 0800 882200. Minicom users may also call. Information is also contained in the *Disability Reports Handbook* published by the Disability Alliance. This handbook is available in most reference libraries.. The RNID also publishes a useful information leaflet on *Social Security Benefits and Deaf People.*

Important benefits include:

- Incapacity benefit; this will replace Invalidity and Sickness Benefit from 13 April 1995.
- Attendance allowance.
- Disability Living Allowance.
- Disability Working Allowance.
- Industrial Injuries Disablement Benefit – a full description of what constitutes 'occupational deafness' is given in the DSS leaflet NI 207. If you think your job has made you deaf.
- War Pensions. To receive a War Disablement Pension due to deafness you must be at least 20 per cent deaf. Total deafness is 100 per cent.

Voluntary Services

The five principal national organizations are the Royal National Institute for Deaf People (RNID); Hearing Concern (The British Association of the Hard of Hearing BAHOH); the British Deaf Association (BDA); the National Deaf Children's Society (NDCS) and the National Association of Deafened People (NADP). In addition, some 27 other organizations are affiliated to the UK Council on Deafness (UKÇOD).

The RNID

The RNID was founded in 1911 as 'the National Bureau for promoting the general Welfare of the Deaf' – 'to become, it is hoped, the centre of information respecting the deaf in these islands'.

Currently, the RNID is the only major charity in the UK concerned with all aspects of hearing impairment representing deaf, deafened, hard of hearing and deaf–blind people. The RNID has described its vision as 'enabling people who are hearing impaired to exercise their right to full citizenship and to enjoy equal opportunities'. It aims to do this by 'increasing awareness and understanding of hearing impairment and people who are hearing impaired and campaigning to remove prejudice and discrimination by raising issues and promoting debate in the press, media and in parliament'. Apart from these pressure group activities the RNID's range of services may be categorized under the following headings:

Information

An enquiry service (0800 413 114); leaflets; current awareness services; the *Soundbarrier* monthly magazine and *Deaf–View* – teletext news for deaf and hard of hearing people. The RNID library is possibly the most comprehensive collection of books and journals on audiology and associated fields in the world.

Training

Community and training for professions; communication courses; vocational training for deaf persons.

Medical

Research clinics at University College Hospital, London for tinnitus, hearing and balance disorders and paediatric audiology; support for the cochlea implant programme.

Tinnitus Support

Co-ordinates the British Tinnitus Association for people with tinnitus which issues a quarterly newsletter and has groups throughout the UK and overseas; the Tinnitus helpline (0345 090210).

Technology

The Technical Awareness Service concerned with testing and comparing hearing/environment aids and other equipment; research on applications of new technology and methods of evaluating hearing impairment.

Communication

A network of interlocking units to provide communication support for people who are deaf or hard of hearing; the Typetalk Telephone Exchange.

Residential

Seven residential or rehabilitation centres for deaf people additionally disadvantaged by age, other physical disabilities or educational, emotional or social pressure.

Marketing

Sound Advantage (0733 361199) is the RNID's marketing service and offers for sale a range of tested and approved environmental aids including listening devices, special telephones and textphones and alarms and altering devices.

The RNID has offices in Manchester, Birmingham, Middlesborough, Bath, London, Belfast and Glasgow. Membership of the RNID requires the payment of an annual minimum subscription and gives the right to vote on elections to the Institute's Council.

Hearing Concern (HC)

Founded in 1947 as the British Association of the Hard of Hearing, Hearing Concern is the national body for those who have hard of hearing usually in post-school life. Its members therefore normal speech and education and use hearing aids and lipreading as their preferred means of communication.

Like the RNID, Hearing Concern acts as a pressure group. It has campaigned on a range of issues including shortcomings in audiology units and hearing aid clinics, shortage of lipreading classes, a national standard for the issue of environmental aids by local authorities and environmental noise.

HC offers a wide range of services. Social activities are based on a national network of affiliated clubs offering friendly company and interesting activities. A National Young People's Committee arranges events that are attractive to younger people with hearing impairments.

Help with hearing aids and other technical devices are monitored by HC's Technical and Telecommunications Committees.

An advanced network of over 100 volunteers offers help on a national basis to first time hearing aid users and those who may experience difficulty in coming to terms with their hearing loss or the use of their hearing aid. Lipreading is encouraged through the Association of Teachers of Lipreading to Adults. Since 1985 Hearing Concern has had total responsibility for the Sympathetic Hearing Scheme.

The BAHOH can be joined in one of two ways. First, membership of an affiliated hard of hearing club carries automatic membership. Second, it is possible for non-club members to become general members. The magazine, published quarterly, is *Hearing Concern.*

The British Deaf Association (BDA)

The BDA was founded in 1890 as the British Deaf and Dumb Association 'to elevate the educational status of the deaf and dumb in the United Kingdom'. It is therefore the oldest national organization for persons who are hearing impaired in the UK. The word 'dumb' was not deleted from its title until 1971. Although it offers its services to all people with a hearing loss the BDA is the grass roots organization of deaf people, with over 18,000 members, almost all of whom are deaf and use sign language. It is they who elect the BDA's governing body, the Executive Council. BDA members are organized into 178 local branches scattered throughout Great Britain and eight regional councils.

The broad aims of the BDA are 'to advance and protect the interests of deaf people, develop pride, identify and leadership qualities and awareness of their rights and responsibilities; thereby strengthening their own community and enabling them to take their place as full members of the wider national community'.

To achieve these aims the BDA manages a programme comprising:

o Sign language service

o Advocacy and Casework services

o Education and Training services

o Youth services

o Sport and leisure services

o Information services.

The BDA is Great Britain's representative to the World Federation of the Deaf and studies current international developments in health, education and welfare. Several useful surveys have been initiated by the BDA. In association with the Durham University Deaf Studies Research Unit the BDA has published the *Dictionary of British Sign Language/English.* Individuals, whether deaf or hearing, can join the BDA but only those who are deaf can vote or stand for election to committees. The Journal of the BDA published monthly is the *British Deaf News.*

The National Deaf Children's Society (NDCS)

The NDCS was formed in 1944 and is the national organization concerned with deaf children. The word 'deaf' in the title is used in the widest sense, applying to all children whose hearing impairment constitutes a handicap. The Society's purpose is to see that children born deaf, or who become deaf at an early age, are enabled to live fulfilling lives. It offers help with the home environment, educational and medical facilities. A Technology Information Centre is maintained in Birmingham.

The NDCS works through regional associations, some of which have a number of branches. The Society welcomes as members, parents, teachers of the deaf, otologists, social workers with deaf people and all active well wishers of deaf children. The NCDS Journal published quarterly is *Talk.*

The National Association of Deafened People (NADP)

The NADP was formed in 1984 by a group of people who had lost their hearing in the prime of life and discovered that their particular needs were not well understood and only partly catered for by existing bodies. The NADP is now a national organization with a rapidly expanding sphere of influence. The Association is very much concerned with rehabilitation, education, training and employment opportunities for deafened people. It has issued a number of useful publications including guides to employment and cochlea implants.

Membership is open to al interested in the aims of the Association. The NADP journal is *Network.*

The UK Council on Deafness (UKCOD)

The UK Council on Deafness was established in 1994 as an organization concerned with bringing together deaf, deaf–blind and hearing impaired communities. As the press release relating to the launch of the Council stated:

> 'Deaf people in their various organisations, have long been campaigning for improved communication with the hearing world. The Council on Deafness will take up this issue, but will also build links between members, enabling these diverse communities to improve communication with each other ...
>
> UKCOD's first priority will be to support the introduction of comprehensive anti-discrimination legislation for disabled people.'

The UK Council on Deafness currently (1995) has 32 members. These are:

Association of Lipspeakers
Association of Teachers of Lipreading to Adults
Breakthrough
British Association of Audiological Scientists
British Association of Otolaryngologists
British Association of Teachers of the Deaf
British Deaf Association
British Society of Hearing Therapists
Catholic Deaf Association

Church of England Committee for Ministry among Deaf People
Council for the Advancement of Communication with Deaf People
Deaf Broadcasting Council
Ewing Foundation
Friends for the Young Deaf
Hard of Hearing Christian Fellowship
Hearing Concern
Hearing Dogs for the Deaf
Hearing Research Trust
Jewish Deaf Association
Link – The British Centre for Deafened People
Méniére's Society
Midland Regional Association for the Deaf
National Association of Deafened People
National Aural Group
National Centre for Cued Speech for the Deaf
National Deaf Children's Society
The Royal Association in Aid of Deaf People
Royal National Institute for Deaf People
The Scottish Association for the Deaf
Sense – the National Deafblind and Rubella Association
South East Regional Association for the Deaf
Wales Council for the Deaf

Appendix 1

The Hearing Aid Council
Code of Practice

Whereas the terms of the following Code of Trade Practice have been approved in writing by the Secretary of State for Trade and Industry:

Now, therefore, the Hearing Aid Council, acting pursuant to Section 1 (3) of the Hearing Aid Council Act 1986 (hereinafter referred to as 'the Act') hereby prescribe the following code of trade practice for adoption from 1 April 1994 by persons registered as dispensers of hearing aids under the Act and by persons employing such dispensers:

Dispensers

1. Dispensers shall not indicate the fact that they are registered under the Act by means of any written representation, advertisement or promotional material involving the use of words other than:

   (a) 'registered hearing aid dispenser'

   (b) 'registered hearing aid dispensers'

   (c) 'RHAD' (to be used only after a name as registered)

   (d) 'registered under the Hearing Aid Council Act 1986'; or

   (e) 'all hearing aid dispensers are required to be registered with the Hearing Aid Council'

2. Dispensers shall maintain at all times a high standard of ethical conduct in the operation of their practice.

3. Dispensers shall at all times give the best possible advice they can to their clients regarding hearing aids and their use.

4. Dispensers shall, where appropriate, make it known to their clients that a hearing aid may not necessarily be of benefit.

5. Dispensers who are not medically qualified shall advise a client to seek medical advice, if he had not already done so. If it appears that the client has been exposed to loud noise in his work or elsewhere or if the client complains of or shows any of the following:

   (a) excessive wax in the ear (whether revealed by examination prior to taking an ear impression or otherwise):

   (b) discharge from the ear;

   (c) dizziness or giddiness (vertigo);

(d) earache;

(e) deafness only of short duration or of sudden onset;

(f) unilateral perceptive deafness;

(g) conductive hearing loss;

(f) tinnitus (ringing or other noises in the ear or ears).

6. Dispensers who are not medically qualified shall not:

    (a) represent themselves in any way as being qualified;

    (b) practise any form of medical or surgical treatment for deafness;

    (c) at any time assume the status of one having surgical or medical knowledge; or

    (d) advertise that they are in a position to cure any human failing or physical ill.

7. Dispensers shall not describe themselves as consultants, or specialists, or audiologists unless immediately preceded by the words, 'Hearing Aid';

8. A dispenser must have available for use at every consultation the following equipment;

    (a) a pure tone audiometer, which contains the facilities for both air and bone conduction audiometry with masking, meeting the requirements of IEC 645–1:1992 'Audiometers, Part 1: Purt-tone audiometers' Type 1, 2 or 3 regularly calibrated with reference to the standards specified in BS2497; 1992 (=ISO 389: 1990) 'Standard reference zero for the calibration of pure tone air conduction audiometers' and BS6950: 1988 (=ISO 7566: 1987) 'Standard reference zero for the calibration of pure tone bone conduction audiometers'; and

    (b) an otoscope and specula together with facilities for cleaning them; and

    (c) suitable aural impression material and associated equipment; and

    (d) a range of air conduction (ear-level and body-warm) hearing aids, and of bone conduction hearing aids.

    A dispenser must also be able to arrange speech audiometry when required.

9. Unless a pure tone audiogram taken within the previous two months by, or under the supervision of an ear, nose and throat specialist is available to the dispenser at the time of consultation appropriate air-conduction and bone-conduction audiometry must be carried out with the use of masking where necessary.

10. Neither a dispenser nor anyone else employed by or acting on behalf of a dispenser or employer of dispensers shall visit any existing client or potential client at his or her home unless the client or an appropriate person acting on his or her behalf has either requested or agreed to a visit in accordance with the following requirements.

(a) The request or agreement was to a visit being made on a particular day. This request or agreement cannot be a prior arrangement under which visits would be made more than 3 months later.

(b) Whenever practicable and appropriate a written notice must have been sent to the client whether existing or potential with the details of the proposed visit including the day, date, approximate time and the name of the dispenser or employer must at that time make a record of why it was not practicable or appropriate to do so and must provide a copy of this record to the Council is so requested.

(c) When the request for a visit occurs as a consequence of an approach by telephone by the dispenser or someone acting on his behalf the written notice must have been sent and must be accompanied by a first class pre-paid card providing the client or potential client with the opportunity to decline or to alter the appointment. The visit must be at least 10 calendar days after the despatch of the notice by first class post.

(d) When the request for a visit occurs as a consequence of a written approach by the dispenser or someone acting on his behalf, the dispenser may visit only where there has been written confirmation of the client's agreement to a visit on that day.

(e) A dispenser or employer of dispensers or anyone else employed by or acting on behalf of a dispenser or employer of dispensers may not charge for a visit or test unless the client has agreed to the proposed charge before the day of the visit. In such instances, a written notice as described at (b) above must have been sent and it must have included details of the proposed charge.

This rule comes into effect on 1st January 1995.

II. Before providing or effecting the supply of a hearing aid or aids or before the client has entered into any commitment if this should be later, dispensers must provide the client in writing with the following;

(a) the make and model of the aid/aids to be supplied; and

(b) any cash price, including VAT for the hearing aid and details of any additional charges and any alternative terms as required by law, if credit terms or rental are offered; and

(c) the precise terms of any trial offered; and

(d) the terms and conditions, if any, under which a client may cancel the order and the terms and details of any refund which may be available; and

(c) the name and address and telephone number of the dispenser and the firm, if different

(i) supplying the hearing aid;

(ii) whom the client should contact to exercise any rights under (c) and (d) above

(iii) whom the client should contact to obtain batteries, repairs or service; and

(f) the terms of any guarantee; and

(g) an undertaking to arrange a further personal consultation with the client at no charge at the place of the original consultation or wherever agreed by the client, within 6 weeks of the supply of the hearing aid/aids, to assess the client's progress and to offer any assistance that may be required; and

(h) a statement that none of the above affect the client's statutory rights; and

(i) a statement that 'All hearing aid dispensers are required to be registered with the Hearing Aid Council and a copy of the Council's duties include ensuring adequate standards in dispensers' conduct and competence. The address is: The Hearing Aid Council, Witan Court, 305 Upper Fourth Street, Central Milton Keynes, MK9 1EH'.

This rule comes into effect on 1st January 1995.

Employers of Dispensers

12. Employers shall ensure that:

(a) all dispensers employed by them comply with the Code of Practice; and

(b) all trainees employed by them only dispense under such supervision as required in the Code of Practice and Standard of Competence; and

(c) any dispensing by trainees employed by them is in accordance with the Code of Practice.

13. Employers shall not indicate the fact that they are registered under the Act or that they employ dispensers registered under the Act by means of any written representation, advertisements or promotional literature involving the use of words other than:

(a) 'registered under the Hearing Aid Council Act 1968;'

(b) 'registered hearing aid dispensers;'

(c) 'all hearing aid dispensers are required to be registered with the Hearing Aid Council'; or

(d) 'all hearing aid dispensers are required to be registered with the Hearing Aid Council'; or

(e) 'all employers of hearing aid dispensers are required to be registered with the Hearing Aid Council.

14. Employers shall not describe dispensers as consultants, or specialists, or audiologists unless immediately preceded by the words 'Hearing Aid'.

Dispensers and Employers of Dispensers

15. Dispensers and employers shall ensure that a copy of this Code of Practice shall be made available to any person requesting it.

16. Dispensers and employers shall not designate any premises as a Clinic or Institute.

17. Dispensers and employers shall not take part directly or indirectly in the making of survey by personal contact or telephone from members of the public regarding deafness or the sale of hearing aids with a view to securing business.

18. Dispensers and employers shall make reasonable provision for the servicing of hearing aids and ancillary equipment supplied by them whether of their own make or not.

19. Dispensers and employers shall give their clients the benefit of any guarantee offered by the manufacturers of the goods. In addition, no guarantee shall derogate from or infringe in any way the client's ordinary legal rights under common or statutory law.

20. Dispensers and employers taking part in any exhibition or public demonstration of hearing aids away from their own permanent places of business (other than trade or medical exhibitions at which aids are not on sale or offer to the public) shall ensure that adequate provision for subsequent refitting and service is available. The full name and registered Head Office address must be prominently displayed.

21. Dispensers and employers shall deal with reasonable expedition and in a proper manner with all enquiries made to them by the Registrar in connection with complaints made to the Council by persons with impaired hearing or any person or organisation acting on their behalf with regard to such complaints.

Supervisors

22. Only those dispensers who have been registered for at least two years may supervise trainees. Dispensers are responsible for any work by a trainee done under their supervision as required in the Code of Practice and Standard of Competence. Dispensers are also responsible for ensuring that any dispensing undertaken by those they supervise is in accordance with this Code of Practice.

23. Dispensers must notify the Registrar of the Council of the names and such other details as may be required of anyone who wishes to undergo full time training under their supervision. The dispenser shall then be known as that person's 'notified supervisor' and that person as that dispenser's 'notified trainee'.

24. Dispensers may not supervise any trainee after the elapse of 30 days from that trainee having fully satisfied the requirements for registration as a hearing aid dispenser as prescribed from time to time in the Standard of Competence.

25. Notified supervisors must:

(a) satisfy themselves that anyone whom they will supervise possesses the appropriate qualifications required by the Standard of Competence; and

(b) ensure that their notified trainees are aware of the requirements for preliminary and post-examinations training as prescribed from time to time in the Standard of Competence; and

(c) ensure that their notified trainees dispense hearing aids only when undergoing full time training; and

(d) either sign a certificate testifying that a notified trainee is ready to sit the Council's examinations as prescribed in the Standard of Competence within two years of that trainee having been notified to the Council or obtain the Council's agreement to that trainee continuing full time training under their supervision; and

(e) either sign a certificate testifying that a notified trainee has satisfactorily completed the post-examination training within nine months of that trainee having been declared successful in all parts of the examination held by the Council or obtain the Council's agreement to that trainee continuing full time training under their supervision.

In the event that the Council does not agree to a trainee continuing full time training as required under (c) and (d) of this rule, then no dispenser may supervise dispensing by that trainee.

26. Notified supervisors must inform the Registrar of any trainee who, for any reason other than registration, ceases to train under their supervision for a period of eight weeks or more.

27. Notified supervisors must ensure that, except as permitted under Rules 28 and 29, their notified trainees:

(a) dispense hearing aids only when under their own physical supervision or under the physical supervision of another supervisor (and for the avoidance of doubt, dispensing includes, but is not restricted to examination of clients, otoscopy, audiometry, ear-impressioning and hearing aid fitting); and

(b) are always described as 'trainees' in dealings with clients.

In the case of trainees notified to the Registrar of the Council before 1st April 1994 part (a) of this Rule takes effect when the results are known of the second 1994 examination held by the Council. Until then:

(i) such trainees shall only be permitted to dispense hearing aids to persons who have been examined in the presence of or by a registered dispenser; and

(ii) the provisions of part (b) of Rule 28 shall apply in the case of such trainees; and

(iii) such trainees' notified supervisors must ensure that any dispensing by such trainees is in accordance with the Code of Practice and that it does not involve the commission of an offence under section 3(2) of the Act.

28. In the case of a trainee who has been declared successful in the Council's written and practical examination as from time to time prescribed in the Standard of Competence, the notified must:

(a) ensure that the trainee undertakes all the normal duties of a dispenser in accordance with the Code of Practice and the Standard of Competence; and

(b) either be available for consultation whenever that trainee dispenses alone or have made prior arrangements with that trainee for a nominated alternative supervisor to be available. The supervisor must arrange to see the client if requested to do so by either the client or the trainee; and

(c) arrange training meetings in accordance with the Standard of Competence; and

(d) provide the trainee with a logbook, in the form prescribed by the Council, and ensure that the trainee maintains the logbook as required in the Standard of Competence; and

(e) ensure that the trainee is described as a 'pre-registered hearing aid dispenser' in dealings with clients.

This Rule does not apply to those trainees who, having been notified to the Registrar of the Council before 1st August 1993, are declared successful in the first 1994 examination held by the Council or to those trainees who, having been notified to the Registrar of the Council before 1st February 1994, are declared successful in the second 1994 examination held by the Council.

29. In the case of a trainee who is an applicant for registration undergoing an adaption period, the notified supervisor must ensure that the applicant:

(a) is aware of the requirements of the Code of Practice and the detailed rules set for the adaption period; and

(b) dispenses under such supervision as set for that trainee's adaptation period; and

(c) has a logbook, in the form prescribed by the Council, and maintains the logbook as required; and

(d) is always described either as a 'trainee' or as an 'overseas applicant for registration' in dealings with clients.

Definitions

30. The following terms have the same meanings in the Hearing Aid Council Act 1968 and accordingly:-

'dispenser of hearing aids' means an individual who conducts or seeks to conduct oral negotiations with a view to effecting the supply of a hearing aid, whether by him or another, to or for the use of a person with impaired hearing; and references to the dispensing of hearing aids or to acting as a dispenser of such aids shall be construed accordingly;

'employer of dispensers' includes any person who enters into any arrangement with an individual whereby that individual undertakes for reward or anticipation of reward to act as a dispenser with a view to promoting the supply of hearing aids by that person – and references to the employing of dispensers and their employment shall be construed accordingly;

'hearing aid' means an instrument intended for use by a person suffering from impaired hearing to assist that person to hear better but does not include any instrument or device designed for use by connecting conductors of electricity to equipment or apparatus provided for the purpose of affording means of telephonic communications:

'prescribed' means prescribed by the rules made by the Council pursuant to section 4 of the Act;

'supply' means supply by way of retail sale or by way of hire; but does not include a sale to a person acquiring for the purposes of trade:

'a trainee' means a person whose name has been notified to the Registrar of the Council in accordance with the provisions of Section 3(1)(a)(ii) of the Act and who is undergoing full time training with a view to being registered as a dispenser of hearing aids.

In addition, in this Code of Practice and in the Standard of Competence:

'the Act' means the Hearing Aid Council Act 1968 as amended by the Hearing Aid Council (Amendment) Act 1989:

'dispenser' means the same as dispenser of hearing aids;

'dispensing' means the same as dispensing of hearing aids;

'employer' means the same as employer of dispensers.

'Standard of Competence' means the standard of competence from time to time adopted by the Council pursuant to Section 1(3) of the Act and any variation thereof.

Notes:

Disciplinary proceedings may be brought against those registered with the Council who breach this Code of Practice.

It is a criminal offence for anyone to dispense hearing aids unless:

o registered with the Council as a dispenser of hearing aids; or

o a trainee acting under the supervision of a registered dispenser.

Appendix 2

RECOMMENDED HEARING INSTRUMENT(S) SUPPLY FORM

No.NF/ 24751

Issued in conformity with the Hearing Aid Council Code of Practice

	Title/Mr/Mrs/Ms/Miss	Name / Address / Telephone of Hearing Aid Supplier
Name of Client and Full Permanent Address		
Post Code	Telephone	

Following evaluation of your hearing, details of the hearing instrument(s) recommended as being suitable are shown below.

Name of Registered Hearing Aid Dispenser (Address / Telephone if different from above)

Make	Type	Model	L / R / Bin / BC

Comments

The instrument(s) will be fitted on the following agreed terms:

Details of any agreed alternative terms:

Instruments(s) Price		Total Cash Price	
Ear mould(s)		Initial Payment	
Extra item(s)		Cash Price Balance	
Total Cash Price		Service Charge	
Deposit		Total Balance Due	
Balance due on delivery		Repayment Period	Months

Please note: Within a period of six weeks from date of supply at least one further personal consultation will be provided without charge, to assess progress and to offer further assistance if required.

In the unlikely event of instrument(s) proving to be unsuitable then providing return is in new condition within.............days of the date of supply, clients only obligation is payment of £....................and any monies paid in excess of this amount will be refunded.

INSTRUMENT GUARANTEE AND SERVICE: The instrument(s) above will be guaranteed against any defect of workmanship or material for a period of............ months from date of purchase. Damage due to misuse, accident or attempted repairs may not be covered by the Guarantee. Interference with the instrument and/or replacement of parts other than by the manufacturers or the manufacturer's authorised agents renders the Guarantee invalid. Service under the terms of Guarantee, and subsequently, will be provided through the Hearing Aid Supplier. None of the foregoing affects the clients statutory rights. All hearing aid dispensers are required to be registered with the Hearing Aid Council and a copy of the Council's Code of Practice may be seen on request. The Council's duties include ensuring adequate standards in dispensers' conduct and competence. The address is:

The Hearing Aid Council, Witan Court, 305 Upper Fourth Street, Central Milton Keynes, MK9 1EH

Signature of Client		Signature of Hearing Aid Dispenser		Date	

Copyright Design, Form RHIS/NF/8/93

Appendix 3

The list of members affiliated to the UK Council on Deafness gives some idea of the number of organizations concerned with various aspects of hearing loss. There are, however, many more. A comprehensive list is contained in the *Information Directory* issued by the RNID which provides information on the address of local, regional and national services concerned with hearing loss including Social Workers, Schools, Further and Higher Education, Advice, Counselling, Communication Services, Services for the Deaf, Blind, Speech and Hearing, Therapists Clubs and Societies, Arts and Leisure and Deaf Drivers.

The address of some organizations may change and it is suggested that apart from the five national organizations listed below up-to-date information on addresses and telephone numbers should be obtained either from RNID Information Service of UKCOD.

The *RNID*:
105 Gower Street, London WC1E 6AH
Telephone: 0171 387 8033 Enquiry Service 0800 413 114
Text: 0171 388 6038 (Qwerty 300 Baud) 071, 383 (Minicom)
Fax: 0171 388 2346

RNID Services
Regional Offices
RNID Midlands
117 Hagley Road
Edgbaston, Birmingham B16 8LB
Tel: 0121 455 6835 (voice/Minicom) 0121 452 1071 (text)
0121 454 1320 (Fax)

RNID North
National Computing Centre, Armstrong House,
Oxford Road, Manchester, M1 7ED
Tel: 0161 242 2316 (voice/Minicom)

RNID North East
Southlands Centre Ormesby Road
Priestfields, Middlesbrough
Cleveland TS3 0HB
Tel: 01642 327583 (voice) 01642 300630 (Minicom)
01642 300935 (Fax)

RNID Northern Ireland
Wilton House, 5 College Square North
Belfast BT1 6AR
Tel: 01232 239619 (voice/Minicom) 01232 312032 (Fax)

RNID South East
39 Store Street
London WC1E 7DB
Tel: 0171 916 4144 (voice/Minicom) 0171 916 4546 (Fax)

RNID South West
13B Church Farm Business Park
Corston, Bath BA2 9AP
Tel: 01225 874460 (voice\Minicom) 01225 874246 (Fax)

Other RNID Services

RNID Library
The Institute of Laryngology and Otology
330—332 Gray's Inn Road
London EC1X 8EE
Tel: 0171 915 1553 (voice) 0171 915 1443 (Minicom)

RNID Medical Research Unit
The Ferens Institute
Middlesex Hospital LAnnexe
3rd Floor, Cleveland Street
London W1P 5FD
Tel: 0171 380 9308 (voice) 0171 580 6726 (Fax)

RNID Science and Technology Unit
105 Gower Street
London WC1E 6AH
Tel: 0171 387 8033 (voice) 0171 383 3154 (Minicom)
0171 388 6038 (Qwerty 300 Baud) 0171 388 2346 (Fax)

Sound Advantage (the RNID's Marketing Service)
1 Metro Centre
Welbeck Way
Peterborough PE2 7UH
Tel: 01733 361 1199 (voice) 01733 238 8020 (text) 01733 361 1161 (Fax)

RNID Tinnitus Helpline
Unit 2, Pelham Court
Pelham Road
Nottingham NG5 4AP
Tel:P 01345 090210 (voice\Minicom)

Typetalk
Pauline Ashley House
Ravenside Retail Park
Speke Road
Liverpool L24 8QB
Tel: 0151 494 1000 (voice) 0151 494 1022 (Fax)
0800 592600 (technical help)
0800 592593 (billing and rebate inquiries)
0800 500888 (registration Telcom Gold 79;BKU 020)

Some other national organizations

Association of Teachers of Lipreading to Adults (ATLA)
c/o The Post Office
Slimbridge, Gloucestershire GL2 7BL

British Deaf Association
38 Victoria Place
Carlisle, Cumbria CA1 1HU
Tel: 01228 48844 (voice/Minicom) 01228 28719 (Qwerty 300 Baud)

The British Tinnitus Association
Room 6, 14–18 Bar Green
Sheffield S1 1DA

Hearing Concern
7–21 Armstrong Road
London W3 7JL
Tel: 0181 743 1110 (voice/Minicom)
0181 742 9043 (Fax)

National Association of Deafened People
Longacre
Horsley's Green
High Wycombe
Bucks HP14 3UX (01494 482355)

The National Centre for Cued Speech for the Deaf
19–30 Watling Street
Canterbury, Kent CT1 2UD
Tel: 01227 450757 (voice/Minicom)

The National Deaf Children's Society
Family Services Centre
Carlton House, 24 Wakefield road
Rothwell Haigh
Leeds, West Yorkshire LS26 0SF
Tel: 0532 823458 (voice/text)

Royal Association in Aid of Deaf People
27 Old Oak Road
London W3 7HN
Tel: 0181 743 6187 (voice/Minicom)

Sense
The National Deaf–Blind and Rubella Association
11–13 Clifton Terrace
London N4 3SR
Tel: 0171 272 7774 (voice/Qwerty) 0171 272 6012 (Fax)
The UK Counsel on Deafness
0181 293 1110

Subject Index

References in italic indicate illustrations

access to work scheme
143, 147
acousticon 78–79
acoustic fan 77
acoustic reflex testing
45–48
acts of Parliament
Chronically Sick and
Disabled Persons Act
1970 151, 166
Companies Act 1985 139
Disability Discrimination
(Bill)142
Disabled Persons
Employment Act 1944
142
Disabled Persons
(Services, Consultation
and Representation)
Act 1986 151
Health and Safety at
Work Act 1974 138
Hearing Aid Council Act
1968 92, 150
Local Authority Social
Services Act 1970 151
National Health Service
Acts 1948 and later
149–150
National Health Service
Act 1946 89
National Health Service
Act 1977 151
National Health Service
and Community Care
Act 1990 151
*Advertising Standards
Authority* 93
air conduction 28, 57
assistive listening devices
105–107
*Association of Teachers of
Lip-reading to Adults* 125
attendance allowance 152
audiograms 28, 38, 52
examples of audiograms
29, 30, 38, 40, 41, 42
interpreting audiograms
38–41
audiometers 25–26
clinical 25
computerisation 27
diagnostic 26
screening 26
audiometric tests 27–48
Bekesey tests 28, 47
bone conduction tests 29
brain stem electric
response 48
evoked response tests 28,
47
impedance tests 28, 41
masking 31
pure tone tests 28–31
speech testing 31–35
Tinnitus markers 64
audiometry 25–48
auditory training 135–136
*BDA (British Deaf
Association)* VIII, 131,
155
Bekesey audiograms 47
bels 25
Bench, Kowal and
Bamford sentence tests
32, 33
bianural hearing 5
biofeedback 19
*Birmingham Resource Centre
for Deafened People* 147
bluffing 72, 73, 74, 126,
143
bone conduction 28, 57
brain stem electric response
audiometry 48
*BAHOH (British Association
of the Hard of Hearing) see
Hearing Concern*
British Code of
Advertising Practice
93–94
British Deaf Sports Council
British Sign Language IX,
131
British Society of Audiology 37
British Tinnitus Association
20, 153

carhart notch 39
cholesteatoma 10
cochlea 3, 16, 41, 42, 47,
48, 59–60, 108, 109
cochlear implants 102,
108–119, 144
assessment of suitability
for 100–111
centres 110

components of 108, 110, 113
definition 108
future of 118–119
implant team 112
lipreading and 124
operation 113
pros and cons of 115–118
the 'Switch on' 113–114
City Lit Centre fr Deaf People 90
computed tomography (CT) scan 112
conductive hearing loss 7, 8, 45, 54–59
conversation aids 104
Council for the Advancement of Communication with Deaf Persons (CACDP)
courage 75–76
cued speech 134–135, 148

Danish mouth–hand system 133–134, 145
Deaf Broadcasting Council X
definitions
decibels 23–25
  admittance 41
  adventitiously deaf VII
  auditory evoked response 47
  binaural hearing 5
  cochlear implant 108
  congenital hearing loss 11
  deaf VII
  deafened VII
  disability 35
  handicap 35
  hard-of-hearing 35
  hereditary hearing loss 11

immittance 41
impairment 35
impedance 41
lipreading 120
Otitis media 9
otosclerosis 10
pre-lingual deafness VII
post-lingual deafness VII
retrocochlear disorder 47
traumatically deafened VII
tympanometry 44
depression 68–69, 70–71
diet 16–17, 60
Disability Alliance 152
Disabled Graduates Career Information Service 143
Disabled Living Foundation 143
disabled living centres 106
disability employment adviser 142
disability living allowance 152
disability symbol 138
disability working allowance 152
drug avoidance (in Tinnitus) 152
dizziness *see* vertigo
drugs
  alcohol 17
  antihistamines 61
  aspirin 16
  caffeine 17
  cortisone 17
  dilatin 18
  diuretics 61
  quinine 17
  serc 13, 61
  sulphonamides 9
  valium 18

vasodilators 61

ear (anatomy) 1–6
  inner 3–4
  middle 2, 4
  outer 1–2
ear drum (tympanum) 2, 4, 51, 54–55
ear trumpets 78, 104
electrocochleography 47
empathy in hearing loss 75
Employers Forum for Disability 139
employment 107, 137–143
environmental aids 104–107
equipment for employment 107
eustachian tube 2, 9, 10, 11, 42, 46, 51, 52, 53, 57
evoked response audiometry 47–48

family relationships 145–148
fenestration 55–56
finger spelling 132–133
free field testing 34
frustration arising from hearing impairment 71–72

glue ear 9, 53
head noises *see* Tinnitus

hearing aids 77–107
advertisments for
alternative to
    Stapedectomy 58
batteries 80, 90, 101, 102
behind the ear 84, 86,
    88, 92
BICROS 84, 87, 92
binaural fitting 90
body worn 85, 88, 92
bone conduction 86
components 79–82
controls 82–84
    automatic gain
        control (AGC) 83,
        87
    dynamic range
        compression
        (DRC) 83
    peak clipping (PC) 83
    telecoil orT switch 84
    tone control (TC) 83
    volume control (VC)
        83
CROS 84, 87, 92, 99
development sin 87
dispensers 92, 93,
    94–96, 100
dynamic range 98
ear mould 79, 81–82, 89
exhibitions 94
faults 103
features 82–84
fitting 97–99
historical devices 77, 78
in the canal 84, 88
in the ear 84, 85–86, 88
insurance 102
learning to use an aid
    99–101
maintaining an aid
    101–102

monaural fitting 98
privately dispensed 92,
    94–96, 99
programmable aids 84
NHS 89–90
spectacle 86, 88
speech reading and
supply form 96
    (Appendix 2)
using
vibro-tactile aid 102
hearing aid centres 90, 94
hearing aid orientation 91,
    99–100, 135
Hearing Aid Council 92–93
    code of practice 93
Hearing Concern (The
    BAHOH) 125, 126,
    153, 154–155
hearing loss
    causes of hearing loss
        7–19
    conductive hearing loss
        7, 8, 9–11, 39, 40
    congenital hearing loss 11
    emotional and
        behavioural effects
        67–76
    hereditary hearing loss 11
    mixed 7
    sensorineural hearing loss
        7, 8, 9, 11–20, 39, 40
Hearing Research Trust 54
hearing tactics 127–129
hearing therapists 90–92,
    136
hearing threshold 28
herbs (in Tinnitus) 17
    Garlic 17
    Gingko Biloba (Chariese
        Maidenhay) 17

Yeast 17
hospitalisation 143–145
hypnotherapy 19

impedance audiometer
    41–44
incapacity benefit 152
industrial injuries
    allowance 152
infection, elimination of
    52–53
Institute of Hearing Research
    VIII 54

Keele, university of 59

link centre for deafened
    people 147
lipreading 120–135
    advantages of 123–124
    basis of 120–122
    cochlear implants and 124
    definition 120
    helping a person to
        120–130
    in practice 126–127
    learning to lip-read
        125–126
    limitations of 12–123
    supplementing 130–136
listening practice 136

Maabaans 14–15
manually coded English
    communication systems
    133–135
measurement of hearing
    disability 35–38

Medical Research Council 33, 54
word lists 33
Menieres disease 8, 12–14, 47, 60–61, 63
minicoms 140
most comfortable loudness level (MCL) 31, 34
myringoplasty 54–55
myringotomy 53

NADP (National Association of Deafened People) 112, 143, 156
NDCS (National Deaf Children's Society) 152, 155–156

occupational deafness 152
ossicles 2, 5, 10, 28, 42, 46, 55–59
ossiculoplasty 55
otitis externa 8
otitis media 8, 9—10, 11, 16, 52
otologist, consulting an 49–50
otosclerosis 10–11, 16, 55–59, 63

PACT (Placing,. Assessment and Counselling Team) 142
palantyne machines 139
pascals 24–25
presybacusis 8, 14–15, 16, 47, 50, 99

RADAR (Royal Association for Disability and Rehabilitation) 143
recruitment 7, 34, 47, 136
register of handicapped persons VII, 150
reissners membrane 4
relaxation (in Tinnitus) 18-20
relaxation tapes 18–19
rinne tuning fork test 51
RNID (Royal National Institute for Deaf Persons) VII, 125, 131, 143, 153–154, 152

sensorineural hearing loss 7, 8
SKILL (The National Bureau for Students with Disabilities) 143
social security benefits 152
society of hearing therapists 91
sound 21–25
  frequency 22
  intensity 22–25
  perception 70
  pitch 22
  'primitive' level 70
  'symbolic' level 79
  warning level 70
sound location 5–6, 136
speech discrimination score (PB) 31, 32
speech discrimination tests 32–35
  Bench, Kowal and Bamford
  Fry
  Boothroyd

medical research council
speech reception threshold (SRT) 31
speech testing 31–35
spondees 31
Schwabach tuning fork test
sign language 130–135
signs supporting English 131
social attitudes to hearing impairments 72–73
speaking tubes 78
sodium flouride therapy 59
speech conservation and improvement 136
stapedectomy 56–58
stapes mobilisation 56
statistics of hearing loss VIII–X
Sympathetic Hearing Scheme 129, 154
symptoms of ear trouble 7, 50
syringing 50

text telephones (minicoms) 139
threshold of discomfort (TD) 31, 34
tinnitus 15–20, 50, 61, 115
  causes 15
  drugs in 17, 62
  maskers 63–66
  relief of 16–2, 62–66
  surgery 63
Tinnitus Helpline 19
Tinnitus support groups 20
tuning fork tests 51–52

tympanograms 45, 46
tympanometry 44–48
tympanoplasty 54
typetalk 139

*UKCOD (UK Council on
    Deafness)* 152, 156–157

vertigo 12, 13, 52, 60
vibro-tactile aids 102
voluntary services
    152–157, Appendix 3

war pensions 152
wax 8, 26, 49, 53, 101
Weber tuning fork test 51
white noise 26
work discrimination scores
    34
world deaf symbol 129
World Federation of the Deaf
    X
World Health Organisation
    35

yoga 20

Author Index

Adler, Alfred 75
Ashley, Jack (Lord) 68, 139
Beales, Philip H 59
Békésy, George Von 14
Bell, Alexander Graham
25, 78
Bench, Kowal and
Bamford 32
Boothroyd, Arthur 33
Corhart, Raymond 97
Corti, Alfrenso 3
Cowper, William 20
Evans, J.D. X
Ewing, Sir Alexander and
Lady 124
Field, D.L. and Haggard,
M.P 128
Fry, D.B. 32
Forchhammer, George 133
Fusfield, I 126, 127
Goffmann, E. 72
Gottesberge, Meyer zum 14
Hazell, J.W.P. 65–66
Heath, Alison 116–118
Hertz, Heinrich, R. 22
Jones, Kyle and Wood
146, 147, 148
Jeffers and Barley 122
Keller, Helen 31
Lempert, Julius
Markides, A 136

Mawson, S.R. 37
McCall, Rosemary 67–68
Meniere, Prosper 12, 16
Meyerson, Lee 69–71
Montrose, Duke of 89
Newall, Alan 139
Pavitt, Laurie 93
Ramsdell, D.A. 70
Rosen, Samuel 14–15, 20,
56
Schuknecht 56
Shambaugh and Scott 59
Shea, John (Jnr) 56
Tate, Maryanne 97–98
Thomas, Lamont and
Morris 137
Vernon, Jack 63–64
Warfield, Frances 73
Wilde, Sir William 54
Wordsworth, William 76
Wullstein, Horst 55